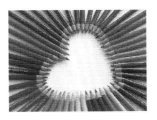

Delighting in the Law of the Lord
A Psalm 119
DevArtJournal
Part I

Delighting in the Law of the Lord
A Psalm 119
DevArtJournal
Part I

Delighting in the Law of the Lord

A Psalm 119
DevArtJournal

Creative Study and Prayer Journal

Part I

Laura R. Brown

4-P Publishing
Chattanooga, TN

Delighting in the Law of the Lord

Psalm 119
DevArtJournal

Scripture taken from the New American Standard Bible unless otherwise noted.
Word study definitions are taken from the Strong's New American Standard Bible Concordance
found on www.blueletterbible.com unless otherwise noted.

First Edition: August 2014
Printed in the United States of America
ISBN: 978-1-941749-00-5

4-P Publishing
Chattanooga, TN

DEDICATION

This book is dedicated to right-brain learners who dare to be different and the left-brain learners who have sincerely thought about it.

Go ahead, you know you want to, color this page!

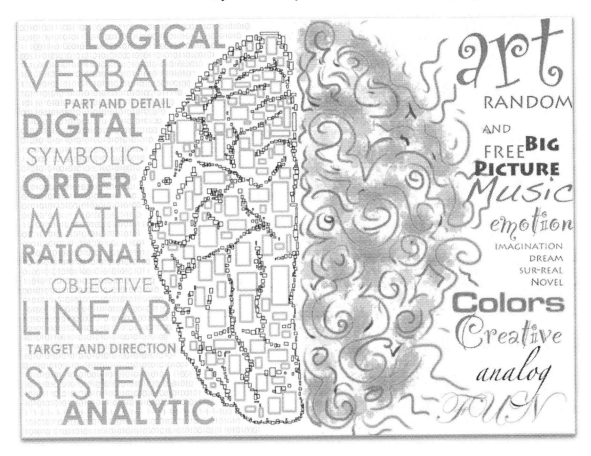

Foreword

I consider it both and honor as well as a privilege to endorse this very fine study of Psalm 119. Within its pages you will find a study that is comprehensive, exhaustive, creative and most of all, interactive. The blessings of the text will come alive in a way never before experienced by each participant of the study as they become thoroughly immersed in a "line upon line, precept upon precept" guide to this wonderful passage of Psalm 119. I highly recommend this engaging study for any Pastor or Group Leader desiring to be able to lead their participants in being able to draw fully from this powerful text as it has been masterfully prepared by the author.

Bishop S. T. Davis, Sr.
Mt. Pleasant Missionary Baptist Church
Winston Salem, NC

Creator, innovator, teacher, minister, visionary and friend; these are all words used to describe Laura Brown, who singlehandedly, I believe, with this book, will change the way meditation, prayer, and journaling is "supposed" to be done! We study the Psalm to gain an understanding of History and an appreciation of worship. Thank God for "right-brained" individuals to have permission to "be"…to create…to be free! This book outlines a practical way to apply Psalm 119 to our modern lives by emphasizing how God is the same yesterday, today and forever. As a Licensed Professional Counselor and Teacher, as well as a Pastor, I appreciate how Laura has married scripture, education, and psychology to enhance the learning experience(s) of those who get a "little" distracted by traditional methods of studying. I urge you to "relax", "relate", "release", and as Laura has encouraged…get your crayons, colored pencils, and a mug of your favorite hot beverage. Open your heart, mind, and ears to what Holy Spirit releases unto you during this study. Enjoy!
Miranda Y. Pearson, LPC, NCC, BCC

Acknowledgements

Above all, I want to thank my Creator God, for sowing seeds of creativity within me. I thank Holy Spirit for guidance through the still small voice that speaks through my doubts and fears. I am grateful for my Savior and Lord, Jesus Christ of Nazareth, and His abiding presence, without which, I can do nothing of value.

I thank my loving husband, Wayne, who has been my greatest supporter and number one fan. I am forever in your debt for your love and friendship.

Thanks to my friends and family who have stood by me and cheered me through this process. Your love and support is beyond value.

A special thanks to the ladies of the Pregnancy Care Center in Ogden, Utah. Tammy, Monica, Kelly and to all the volunteers, who are too numerous to mention.
Your love and support during my assignment in Utah allowed me to discover my gifts and to flourish.

Thanks to Dr. David Banks, my pastor, mentor, and teacher. Your support and encouragement has proven invaluable to me and this project. Thank you for encouraging me to "write that down".

I am grateful for my volunteer team of editors who gave of their time and talents: Monica Allen, Sylvia Banks, Sherwood Davis, Miranda Pearson, Kelly Sampson and Marion & Deana Williams. I love you all!

Thanks to my S.W.A.T. Camp group for reigniting the fire within me and keeping the coals hot!

If I have forgotten anyone, please charge it to my head (the right side, of course) and not my heart!

CONTENTS

Preface

What is a DevArtJournal?

The Psalm 119 DevArtJournal is a weekly Bible study, devotional, creative journal and prayer guide designed to assist you in getting a basic overview of the Psalm. It has intellectual, spiritual, and creative elements designed to keep the reader engaged with the text. Whether you are a seasoned student of the Word, a new believer, or somewhere in between, you will find this study useful in your private time with the Word of God. It is designed to be used as a private devotional or in a group study and prayer setting. If you or your study group are ready to see your Bible study and prayer time take a unique and creative voyage, this is the study for you!

Why a DevArtJournal?

I once felt like a spiritual failure when I listened to others talk about how much they enjoyed their quiet time. My quiet times were a struggle to stay focused. After a few moments of quiet my mind would drift to my laundry list of things to do. I felt that somehow I was not doing it "right". I thought I was a disappointment to God because I didn't look forward to quiet times with the zeal of others. Once I discovered the beauty of adding color, creativity, and art to my study and prayer time, my time with God and His word evolved into a colorful and sometimes quirky adventure. I wrote this book because, as a visual and kinesthetic learner who is easily bored with linear methods, I wanted something that would engage people on various levels of their learning styles.

Who Needs a DevArtJournal?

If you are one who enjoys variety in your study time you will find this study to be engaging. I found most bible studies to be more of what the writer has studied, versus the reader actively investigating the text and drawing thought-out conclusions and personal applications. Some devotionals tend to be a regurgitation of the writer's quiet time revelation without work on the reader's part to actually study the text. Prayer books are typically a collection of other people's prayers. While these forms are inspirational they lacked the personal satisfaction of actively engaging and investigating the word personally. I wanted this study to be a time of active observation, investigative research, personal application, creative stimulation, and prayerful consideration. This study is designed to captivate the reader's attention and motivate to action. If you've grown weary of the usual bible study patterns, this book is for you.

What is the DevArtJournal Community?

The DevArtJournal community is an online meeting spot for the readers of this book. This is where you can see and share creative experiences with others. You will be able to ask questions, have discussions, and even upload your artwork to share with others. This is also a place to connect with me. I would love to see the creative manifestations of your experiences with the Psalm 119 DevArtJournal and get suggestions for other DevArtJournal experiences. Perhaps one of your creations will be featured in upcoming DevArtJournal studies! Take a moment and go to **www.coachlaurabrown.com** to join the DevArtJournal community today.

Introduction

How to Use This Book

Although you can use the Psalm 119 study guide for your personal study time, I recommend finding a friend or starting a small group study to get the most out of this study. Sharing your thoughts and works of art with others will add a rich dimension to your time with Psalm 119. You can join the online DevArtJournal community to see and share creative experiences at **www.coachlaurabrown.com.** You will also find other resources to assist you as you work through the study. You should set aside at least 30 minutes a day to work on the questions in each session instead of trying to finish each session in one sitting.

When doing this with a group you should complete the questions and DevArtJounal pages before you meet with the group. If you are leading the study, I suggest each member receive a copy of the book at least two to four weeks before the study begins. This will give each person time to explore the book and read the preparatory portions of the study. During group sessions the group leader will decide how many of the questions to discuss during the session and how to approach the group prayer time. Two hours should be adequate time. Go to **www.coachlaurabrown** to download the free leader's guide. This will give you more ideas regarding facilitating a group study using the Psalm 119 DevArtJournal.

Be led by Holy Spirit as you pray. I have only given a basic prayer focus, as I believe Holy Spirit will speak to each person according to their needs versus a prayer according to my needs.

Before beginning each day, pray that your spiritual ears are attentive to the voice of God. Remember, the prayer focus is only a basic guide. Remain open to Holy Spirit's guidance during prayer. Your only desire should be to pray according to the heart, word, and will of God.

Psalm 19:14
14 Let the words of my mouth and the meditation of my heart be acceptable in Your sight, O Lord, my strength and my Redeemer.

What to Expect
Every session title page has the Hebrew alphabet and its corresponding Hebraic symbol. These are fun to try to remember.

- Each session begins with general questions that relate to the stanza you will be studying.

- Each stanza is included. You will find charts in the appendix to record what you learn about the different words used to refer to the law and to record stanza themes. These are optional yet very helpful in this study.

- You will encounter observation questions that require you to write answers directly from the text.

- You will find investigation questions requiring you to use several scripture cross references to answer.

- There will be personal application questions requiring you to connect what you have learned to how you should be living.

- There are word study boxes to aid you in understanding the original meaning of some Hebrew and Greek words. They also give added insight to assist you when answering the questions. If you would like to do your own word studies, I have included a word study instruction sheet, an example of a completed word study, and a blank worksheet that can be duplicated. You can also receive a copy of a blank worksheet by going to my website: **www.coachlaurabrown.com.**

- Some sessions will have creative application activity questions.

- At the end of each session you will find a DevArtJournal page. It is a devotional, art and journal page wrapped up in one. There will be various creative activities for you to do that will incorporate what you have studied. With that in mind, keep some colored pens and pencils handy!

- You will also have a space to journal any additional thoughts, insights, or prayer that come to mind. Sometimes you will find a question to prompt your thoughts.

- The appendix includes many extras: word study instructions, other scriptures that are good to use with creative prayer, a list of recommended books and references, on-line study references and more. Make sure you visit this section.

Visual Clues

 This symbol represents optional creative challenge moments.

 This symbol represents optional critical thinking challenges.

This is a word study box. All word studies in this book are taken from www.blueletterbible.org.

This symbol indicates a Word Study assignment. There is a blank word study sheet located in the appendix.

 This symbol indicates Diving Deeper moments. They will challenge you to go deeper into a topic on your own.

 This symbol represent boxes that contain information related to the study. They do not require any action other than reading the information.

Supply List

- A Bible (the NASB version is used in this study unless otherwise noted).

- Regular and colored pens, pencils, markers or crayons.

- A bible concordance or dictionary. I recommend using an internet version such as **www.blueletterbible.org**

- Instrumental CD (optional). I have listed a few of my favorites in the appendix.

- A notebook (lined or unlined) (optional).

Creative Prayer

The idea of creative prayer combines elements of the ancient practice of *Lectio Divina* with the use of artistic expression. *Lectio Divina* refers in Latin to the practice of "divine reading." A passage of scripture is chosen and a person would then meditate on the passage until they feel their time is complete. Instructions will encourage you to sit still, embrace silence, assume an erect posture, and any other ideas that are counter-intuitive to a kinesthetic learner. There are several steps used in the practice of *Lectio Divina* which will be explained. One major concern about *Lectio Divina* is it doesn't involve actual study of the passage and is based on feeling and emptying your mind rather than sound understanding of scripture. In the ***Psalm 119 DevArtJournal*** you will encounter Creative Prayer, which I call ***"DevArtio"***. This will be done only after spending time observing, investigating, comprehending and applying scripture. This is done with colored pens, pencils, crayons, markers or whatever medium you desire.

What is Creative Prayer?

The idea of Creative Prayer is not to empty your mind but to keep your mind engaged on the passage. For many of us "right-brain" or kinesthetic learners, to ask us to sit in silence and think is an open invitation to distraction. Our minds eventually wander to our grocery list or things left undone, such as laundry or that piece of lint on the floor. With Creative Prayer, your mind, your heart and your hands are simultaneously engaged with the text to combat distraction and allow for creative expression. It takes practice, and may seem awkward at first but you will begin to appreciate the beauty of your time with God and another bonus is you will have a colorful visual representation to refer back to in the future. Your colored pens and pencils become your voice and your prayers become works of art that can prompt you to relive that moment over and over. There are five steps to Creative Prayer or DevArtio:

1. **Record -** Write the passage you are studying. In this study the passage has been typed on the DevArtJournal pages for you but you are welcome to rewrite it.

2. **Read–** Slowly begin reading the selected biblical passage. Read the passage repeatedly until you hear a word or phrase that touches you, resonates, attracts or convicts you. You can read silently or aloud.

3. **Reflect–** Write or circle the word or phrase and ponder it for a few minutes. Listen for what the word or phrase is saying to you at this moment in your life. Think about all you have learned during your study time. As you are meditating on the passage you will be using your colored pens or pencils to draw shapes, lines, images or even other words to keep you connected. Draw around one of the words, ask questions, and listen for a response from Holy Spirit. You may receive a message of comfort, conviction, or exhortation. Write it down on the page. If an image comes to you and you want to express it, then feel free to do so. Don't get caught up in the perfection of the picture. If a person comes to mind write their name and pray for them. When you feel you are finished with that word, move on to the next

word and repeat. (Take as long with this part as you desire). I have included several DevArtio examples throughout the book and in the appendix.

4. **Release and Respond-** When you have completed the reflection portion it's time to release your words to God. This is your time to verbally communicate with Abba. You may offer words of adoration, thanksgiving, repentance, or promises to act upon what has been impressed upon your spirit. You may have questions that you seek an answer to from your time with the chosen word or phrase. There is no wrong way to experience this.

5. **Rest**– Allow yourself to simply rest silently with God, for a time, in the quietness of your heart. Once again, if you find yourself getting distracted, pick up a pen and begin drawing random lines to keep your heart and mind engaged in the process.

Adapted from *Praying in Color*. (MacBeth 2007) For more information about praying in color I highly recommend the book *Praying in Color* by Sybil MacBeth.

Creative Prayer with a Group

In order to practice creative prayer in a group, have the group prepare in unity. This may mean a few moments of silence or listening to a worship or instrumental song. I recommend having soft instrumental music in the background because lyrics tend to distract our minds. I have listed a few recommendations for instrumental "soaking" music in the appendix.

There are different ways to do this as a group. Be flexible. Be Creative. One variation is to have someone read the passage aloud, twice, in a slow and deliberate pace. Pause for a moment between readings and read the passage more slowly the second time.

During the first reading let the group just sit and listen.

For the second reading, invite persons to listen for a word or a phrase that resonates with them. Ask each member to write the word or phrase on their paper. Each person would then complete steps 3-4, silently, on their own. Set a time limit for this part.

After personal times of prayer, allow those who would like to share their experience and drawing with the group. End with a group prayer, each person adding to the prayer something that they wrote or expressed in their personal time.

If you desire, you can end this time with a moment of silence, then release a small prayer of blessing over each member.

If you would like to receive a copy of a leader's study guide please visit my website: **www.coachlaurabrown.com.**

I pray this **DevArtJournal** proves to be a blessing to you and/or your small group.

In The Father's Love,

Laura

(Special note from the author: stick figures are definitely allowed.)

Session One

The Mosaic Law

It's Meaning, Origin, and Purpose

Creativity Page

You will find these blank pages located throughout the book. Use them to: take notes, as extra art pages, or to doodle while you wait for your small group to start. Consider them my gift to you! They are your pages and you are FREE to use them as you wish. You will also find some DevArtio examples on some these pages.

What is your view on the relevance or relationship of Old Testament Laws and the New Testament Believer? Consider the following questions as you write your answer.

Are all of the Old Testament laws still in effect today?

Are only some of the Old Testament laws still relevant?

Which ones do you think are still relevant?

On what do you base your views? Are you confused about which ones are relevant and which ones are not relevant? Don't worry about being right or wrong, this is simply gauging you views before you begin the study.

W hen most people hear the word "law" when it comes to biblical references, typically they think about the Ten Commandments handed to Moses on Mount Sinai. While those commandments are part of the law of the Old Testament they do not encompass all of the laws of the Old Testament. Exodus, Leviticus, and Deuteronomy, contain 613 laws or commands. 365 negative (what you shouldn't do) and 248 positive (what you should do). They are traditionally divided into three categories: moral, social and ceremonial.

Are you ready to discover some valuable information about the Law of God? We will be learning about and discussing such things as the origin of the Law. A few other topics we will discuss will be the function, nature, and purpose of the Law in the Old Testament, as well as the New Testament. I want to tackle these subjects before we get into Psalm 119 because they will help you to better understand the mindset of the psalmist and his relationship with the Law and a how a follower of Jesus should relate to the Law.

Let us be like the Bereans in the New Testament who "... were more noble-minded than those in Thessalonica, for they received the word with great eagerness, examining the Scriptures daily *to see* whether these things were so." (Acts 17:11)

"Father, we pray that we may discover wonderful truths from your word. We ask that you give us wisdom and discernment from on High. We come with fertile hearts and minds prepared to receive the Holy Seed of your Word that it may take root and bear fruit one-hundred fold. In Jesus' name. Amen."

Overview of

Old Testament Laws

Moral Laws

Exodus 20:1-17

Governed moral life; guided Israel in principle of right and wrong in regards to God and man.

Social Law-

Exodus 21:1-23:13

Governed Israel in secular, social, economic and political life

Ceremonial Law

Exodus 25-31; Leviticus

Religious law that guided Israel in worship and spiritual relationship and fellowship with God. It includes the priesthood, tabernacle, and sacrifices.

Deuteronomy contains repeated versions of above laws.

(Bible.org n.d.)

Use this space write your own desire for your study time with Psalm 119

The Law: It's Meaning, Origin, and Purpose

A quick word study using **www.blueletterbible.org** will give the general Hebrew meaning and translations of the word Law. In the Strong's Concordance it is assigned the number H8451 (we will discuss more about word studies later). According to the entry found, the word *towrah* pronounced "Torah", is used 219 times in the Old Testament. It means direction, instruction, legal directives, and codes of law, custom or manners. It comes from the root word "yarah", which means to throw, cast, shoot (like arrows), point out, show, direct, teach, or instruct. In essence, laws are a system of principles or instructions given by one to another. Wow, what an abundance of revelation from such a small word!

1. Using the above information, write your own definition for the word law.

Read: Exodus 20:1; Deuteronomy 5:1-5, 22, 27, 31-33 *and answer the following questions.*

2. Who or What was the source of the Law?

3. For whom was the Law specifically created?

Read: Numbers 15:13-16; Leviticus 24:22

4. What was the expectation of those who were not Israelites in regards to obeying the laws, statutes, and judgments set in place by the LORD?

Alien: H1616

I. sojourner

A. a temporary inhabitant, a newcomer lacking inherited rights

B. of foreigners in Israel, though conceded rights

When God said "let us make man in our image and likeness" he used the words "tselem" and "dĕmuwth". Note that in the Hebrew language these word are given male and female noun genders. That has nothing to do with physical gender. Male and female noun classification denote function or character. Male nouns are typically characterized by what the noun is expected to do and female groupings are characterized by what the noun is expected to be. Why? It is thought to be because men are associated with the external, objective aspect of "doing" things and women are associated with the more subjective, internal aspect of "being".

Therefore, when we see the combination of image and likeness we should understand God's original desire and design was for mankind to function externally and internally as He would. He wants us to "do" as He does and to "be" as He is. Numerous times He exhorts us to "be holy for He is holy". If it were not possible He would not have commanded us to do so.

His laws and commands give us direction to His standard of holiness because they all flow from His divine image and likeness. Each of the 613 laws, commands and statutes can give insight into His nature. Of course we cannot do this on our own. We need help and God had a plan for that also. In the next session we will dig a little deeper into that. Just remember, EVERY law was connected to an aspect of His nature.

Read: Deuteronomy 5:31-33, and answer the following questions.

5.   What reason did God give for creating such laws for the Children of Israel?

Read: Genesis 1:26-27, 31; Leviticus 20:7-9, 22- 26; 11- 43-44; Deuteronomy 7:6

6.   In regards to obeying the commands of the LORD, what seems to be a recurring theme in the above verses?

Read: Exodus. 19:3-6; Deuteronomy. 4:4-8; 26:18

7.   What was special about receiving such commandments from God?

Read: *Genesis 22:17-18; 26:1-5*

8. What kind of law existed before the Mosaic Law? (Explain your answer taking into consideration that the meaning of the word law is simply a system of rules or principle given to guide the conduct of the lives of those who receive those laws).

9. Can you think of the first time in OT history that a system of rules were set in place to guide the conduct of people? What were the commandments and the conditions and consequences? Explain your answer *(hint: there were only TWO people at this time).*

Diving Deeper- Do some research on the Noahide Laws. Share what you discover!

Read: *Exodus 19:7-8*

10. How likely or reasonable is it that any person would remember and obey 613 commandments? Why?

If we were to do a deeper study of all the laws, commands, and statutes we would discover some heavy penalties for disobedience. Working on the Sabbath meant certain death (Exodus 31:14-15; Numbers 15:32-36). Disobeying your parents was cause for capital punishment (Deuteronomy 21:18-21). Excommunication and isolation were common threads in administering correction and consequences. There are several other areas in each division of the law, moral, ceremonial, and social, where the results of disobedience were immediate and/or deadly.

Let us take a look at a passage that sums up the blessings of obedience and the consequences of disobedience to the laws, commands and statutes of the LORD. When studying some passages it is helpful to create a list to keep track of all the information contained within that passage. We are going to make a list to help compare and contrast the blessings and curses associated with the 613 laws the children of Israel were given as they were positioned to enter the land of Canaan.

Read: *Deuteronomy 28:1-68*

11. Make a list of at least ten blessings and curses attached to the Mosaic Law. Summarize your thoughts about your list.

Blessings	Curses

DevArtJournal

Take a moment travel back in time and place yourself in the shoes of the Children of Israel at the time they received these commandments (all 613 of them). How would you feel? When answering, consider they were told how special they were in God's eyes. Consider the blessings and the consequences associated with those laws. In what ways do you think those conditions affected the hearts and minds of the Children of Israel and their descendants.

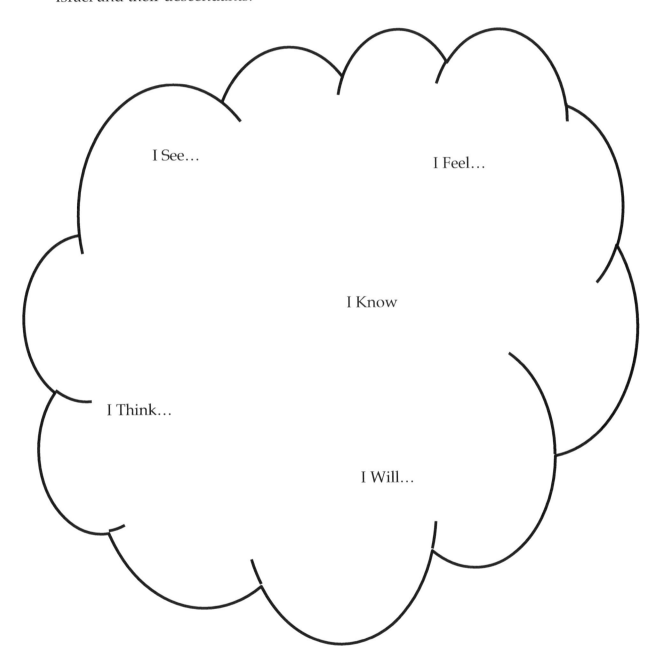

I See…

I Feel…

I Know

I Think…

I Will…

I Love Your Law?

There is more we could learn about the Law from the Old Testament. What you have studied so far will give you a general understanding of the mind, heart, and belief of the writer of Psalm 119. The entire Psalm extols the virtues of the law and the love he has for God's laws. Take this time to think about all that you have discovered thus far. Would you have the same feelings about the Laws and commands of the LORD as the writer of Psalm 119? Why or why not?

Session Two

Old Testament Law and the New Testament Believer

Creativity Page

In our last session we took a brief look at the origin of the Mosaic Laws and their relevance to the Children of Israel and their descendants. We now possess a greater understanding of God's law in relation to a New Testament follower of Christ. During the last session we learned every command, law, and statute flowed from the holy and divine nature of God and He desired them to be followed. We also learned there were consequences, some quite severe, to disobeying. When reading about the ceremonial laws we discovered that God had methods in place in the likely event that the laws were broken in order to restore the relationship between mankind and Himself. Those methods often required the blood sacrifice of a living animal for atonement.

I want to discuss how all that relates to the New Testament follower of Jesus Christ. How should we approach and relate to those 613 laws, commands and statutes? How can we process the punitive nature of the law through the lenses of faith and grace? Grab your pens, pencils and a bible (and perhaps a large cup of coffee or tea) and join me to discover the answers to those questions. Go ahead, I'll wait right here for you!

Getting Started

☐ Take a moment to think about the original design and purpose of the telephone and compare that to its design and usage today. What is the same? What is different? How has that difference affected our relationship with the telephone? Making a list or mind map can help sort the answers. I have provided a sample table for you to organize your thoughts. Feel free to use this one or create your own on the blank page provided for your creative use.

Telephone Time Capsule

Original Design/Purpose	Same	Different	Effect

Telephone Time Capsule

Use this page to write or draw your answer to the "getting started" question on the previous page. Try using a Venn Diagram. More information on Venn Diagrams can be found in the Appendix on page 167. Remember to go to DevArtJournal community on my website, **www.coachlaurabrown,** com to see and share drawings.

What does the evolution of the telephone have to do with the Law and the New Testament believer? (Stick around and it will become clear how the two are related). We will now see what the New Testament has to say about the Mosaic Laws.

Read: *Galatians 3:10; 12; James 2:1, 8-11*

1. Even though we see that the Law had three major divisions, moral, ceremonial, and social laws, what points do the above passages make in regard to our obligation to all of the laws?

His laws and commands give us direction to His standard of holiness and righteousness because they all flow from His divine image and likeness. Each of the 613 laws, commands and statutes can give insight into His nature. Of course we cannot do this on our own. We need help and God had a plan for that also. (Deuteronomy 4:8; Psalm 19:7-9; Romans 7:12-14)

Read: *Roman 8:1-4*

2. What has happened to the original punitive (punishment) nature of the law?

FYI

In the New Testament the word "law" is "nomos" which means a custom, command, anything established, a law or rule producing a state approved of God or by the observance of which is approved of God or a rule that governs one's action. It is used 197 times in the New Testament.

Read: *Romans 3:19-28, 31, 10:4; Galatians 3:19-24, 5:18; Matthew 5:17*

3. What is our new relationship with the Mosaic Law?

4. How is this relationship established?

Read: *Romans 6:14; Romans 7:1-6, 8:2-8; Galatians 2:19*

6. What are the characteristics of this new relationship with the Law? *(This might be a good place to make a list.)*

Read: *Romans 8:14-16; Galatian 5:17; II Corinthians 1:21-22; Ephesian 1:13-14; I John 3:19-24*

7. What role does Holy Spirit play in regards to assisting believers in maintaining this new relationship? How is this accomplished?

CHALLENGE
Read: Roman 2:27-29, 7:6; II Corinthians 3:6 Explain the difference between the "Letter of the Law" and the "Spirit of the Law".

Remember I asked you in the beginning of this session to think about the original design and purpose of the telephone and compare that to its design and usage today. In the same way, I want you to compare the relationship of the Children of Israel and the Mosaic Law to our relationship, as New Testament believers, to the Mosaic Law. I have given you a diagram to simplify the explanation for the Old Testament. Your assignment is to create a diagram, (you choose the form), that explains how New Testament believers in Jesus Christ should relate to the Mosaic laws. Don't panic! I have provided scriptures to assist you. Make it as simple or elaborate as you like. The only requirement is you must be able to explain it to someone else. Here are a few ideas: Use the format below to explain New Testament relationship; create a chart comparing the letter of the law vs. the spirit of the law; use a Venn diagram (see page 167 in the appendix) to contrast and compare the two.

Old Testament

Moral Laws (Exodus 20:1-17)

Provided the standard of righteousness based on the holy nature of God

Reminded them of the weakness and inability of the flesh to be righteous without help from God

Drove them to the ceremonial laws

Ceremonial Laws (Exodus 25-31; Leviticus)

Provided a method of reconcilliation and redemption through faith in blood sacrifices when moral law was violated

Provided instructions on the standard of their spiritual relationship with God

Social Laws (Exodus 21:1-23:13)

Guided Israel on how to live with one another and to expereince a covenant relationship with God through righteous fellowship with man socially, politically, and economically

Relationship Matrix

Using the following headings and scriptures, create a diagram to explain the relationship of the New Testament believer in Jesus Christ with the Mosaic Laws. Feel free to go to DevArtJournal community at **www.coachlaurabrown.com** and share your work.

Moral Laws: Matthew 22:36-38; Romans 8:1-4; Galatians 5:18, 3:1-3, 10-13
Ceremonial Laws: Colossians 2:8-15; Acts 3:19; Romans 10:9-13
Social Laws: Matthew 22:39-40; Galatians 5:22; Roman 13:8-10

Wrapping it Up

This brings us to the conclusion of this session. I truly pray, my friend, that what you have discovered thus far has been enlightening, enriching, and encouraging. This has by no means been an exhaustive study of the Mosaic Law. There is much more that we could discover about the beauty and richness of the Law of the LORD. My prayer is that you have discovered enough to pique your curiosity and motivate you to dig a little deeper on your own. An excellent resource on Mosaic Law can be found at the following web site: **www.bible.org/article/mosaic-law-its-function-and-purpose-new-testament.**

As we have taken our journey to this point, I hope you agree that the final conclusion is the "Law of the Lord" is good for those who use it for good (I Timothy 1:8-11). The law was created and given to forge a righteous relationship between a holy God and sinful man. It serves to teach us about the nature and character of God. It reveals His holiness and His mercy while also revealing the weakness and inability of our flesh to secure our own righteousness and redemption. It shows us our need for redemption through a blood sacrifice. Unlike the Children of Israel, who had to make continual sacrifices on a regular basis, our redemption was paid for once and for ALL through the sacrificial Lamb of God, Jesus Christ.

"But when Christ appeared as a high priest of the good things to come, He entered through the greater and more perfect tabernacle, not made with hands, that is to say, not of this creation; 12 and not through the blood of goats and calves, but through His own blood, He entered the holy place once for all, having obtained eternal redemption. 13 For if the blood of goats and bulls and the ashes of a heifer sprinkling those who have been defiled sanctify for the cleansing of the flesh, 14 how much more will the blood of Christ, who through the eternal Spirit offered Himself without blemish to God, cleanse your conscience from dead works to serve the living God?" (Hebrews 9:11-14 NASB)

As we enter further into this study I want you to remember what you have discovered. As you read, study, and pray through Psalm 119, I want you to read it with a couple of things in the forefront of your mind.

- Read with the intent of understanding how the writer of the Psalm would relate to what he understood about law.
- I also want you to process Psalm 119 through your understanding and relationship as a believer in Jesus Christ.

Remember, God's standard of holiness has not changed. He still hates sin. The method of reconciliation and redemption has changed. Thanks be to the Lord, Jesus Christ. We are now exhorted to live by the "Spirit of the Law" verses the "Letter of the Law". There are some laws that we can no longer live by the letter because of historical, cultural, and geographical changes, yet the spirit of those laws still remain; the spirit that points to an aspect of God's character contained within those specific laws.

If you have gotten this far in the study and you are not yet a believer, then my friend, there is no time like the present to change your relationship with our Heavenly Father. If you do not know Jesus Christ as your Savior and Lord this is your opportunity to receive His grace, mercy and promise of eternal life.

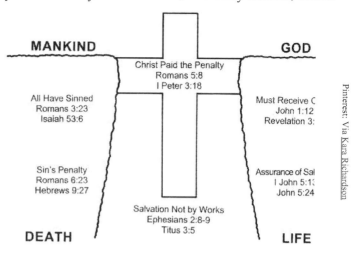

"But *what does it say? "THE WORD IS NEAR YOU, IN YOUR MOUTH AND IN YOUR HEART"--that is, the word of faith which we are preaching, ⁹ that if you confess with your mouth Jesus as Lord, and believe in your heart that God raised Him from the dead, you will be saved; ¹⁰ for with the heart a person believes, resulting in righteousness, and with the mouth he confesses, resulting in salvation. ¹¹ For the Scripture says, "WHOEVER BELIEVES IN HIM WILL NOT BE DISAPPOINTED." ¹² For there is no distinction between Jew and Greek; for the same Lord is Lord of all, abounding in riches for all who call on Him; ¹³ for "WHOEVER WILL CALL ON THE NAME OF THE LORD WILL BE SAVED."" Romans 10:8-13.*

Whether you are already a believer and just want to renew your commitment or you wish to accept the offer of a new life in Jesus Christ, please join me in this prayer:

Dear Father in heaven, I come to you in the name of Jesus. I acknowledge to you that I am a sinner, and I am sorry for my sins and the life that I have lived; I need your forgiveness. I believe that your only begotten Son Jesus Christ shed His precious blood on the cross at Calvary and died for my sins, and I am now willing to turn from my sin. You said in Your Holy Word, Romans 10:9 that if we confess the Lord our God and believe in our hearts that God raised Jesus from the dead, we shall be saved. Right now I confess Jesus as the Lord of my soul. With my heart, I believe that You raised Jesus from the dead. This very moment I accept Jesus Christ as my Savior and according to His Word, right now I am saved.

Thank you Jesus for dying for me and giving me eternal life. Thank you, Jesus, for your grace which has saved me from my sins. I thank you, Jesus, that your grace doesn't give me freedom to sin, but leads me to repentance. Lord Jesus, transform my life that I may bring glory and honor to you. Amen.

If you decided to repent of your sins and receive Christ today, welcome to God's family. As a way to mature in your relationship with Him, I want you to follow up on your commitment. Tell someone else about your new faith in Christ. Spend time with God each day. Seek fellowship with other followers of Jesus. Find a local church where you can worship God and learn more about God. If you prayed this prayer of salvation let me know so I can pray for you. Send me an email at: **coachlaurabrown@gmail.com**

I look forward to our next session as we begin Psalm 119. Until then, be blessed and stay encouraged.

Take a moment to visit **www.coachlaurabrown.com** to join the DevArtJournal community and get access to other resources available, such as a leader's guide, word study worksheets, and more. This is also a good place to connect with me as you are working through the study.

Notes

Creativity Page

Session Three

ALEPH

ב

Creativity Page

Getting started With Psalm 119

Welcome back! Now that we have discovered some important facts about God's law, we can begin to look at what the writer of Psalm 119 had to say about the Law. Remember, he could only write from the perspective of the knowledge that was revealed to him at that time. We now have a greater revelation and should read and study Psalm 119 with that enhanced perspective. I am not suggesting it makes us superior to our Old Testament forefathers in any way, yet it does give us a different viewpoint for the journey.

Before I begin any trip, the most common thing for me to do is to get a map or to proceed to the internet to review and research our destination. I do this to get grand overview of where we are going, the sights we may want to visit along the way and to build excitement for our trip. When making plans to visit Disney World for Christmas with my granddaughter, who was six at that time, we gave her a child's travel guide. She excitedly went through and checked all the sights and rides she wanted to see while there. When we arrived she knew what she was looking for and what she hoped to experience. She reviewed her book nightly and carried it around each day.

We want to approach Psalm 119 in the same way. Let's begin by getting a grand overview of some things you should know and what you will encounter along the way. Grab your pens, pencils, or crayons and join me as we take a closer look at Psalm 119.

Did You Know?

➢ The authorship of Psalm 119 is divided between scholars who say King David wrote it and those who attribute it to Ezra the scribe.

➢ Psalm 119 is the longest chapter in the Bible with 176 verses.

➢ The purpose of this Psalm is to celebrate God's word and instruction to his people.

➢ Psalm 119 is an abecedarian acrostic.

  o **Abecedarian**\ˌā-bē-sē-ˈder-ē-ən\: of or pertaining to the alphabet; arranged in alphabetical order.

  o **Acrostic:** a series of lines or verses in which the first, last, or other particular letters when taken in order spell out a word, phrase, or some other specific meaning

➢ Psalm 119 contains 22 stanzas, each starting with a different letter in the Hebrew alphabet. Each stanza has 8 verses with two lines each.

➢ Each verse makes a commentary regarding the importance of God's law by using various words which denote different characteristics: i.e. testimonies, precepts, statutes, commandments, judgments, ordinances, word, and ways. (NASB)

Getting Started

☐ When embarking upon a new journey to an unfamiliar place, do you prefer using a road map, a GPS, written directions, or just "winging it"? Why?

☐ When you are traveling and realize that you are lost, what is your response?

Read Psalm 119:1-8 – *Circle, highlight or underline each word that refers to the law. (I suggest using a different color for each one. The colors will help you locate the words if you forget to record them on the Law Table in the appendix on page 163).* **Do this for each stanza.** *I have underlined the first set of words below to get you started. Now, it's your turn to color code them if you desire.*

[1] How blessed are those whose way is blameless, who walk in the law of the Lord.
[2] How blessed are those who observe His testimonies, who seek Him with all their heart.
[3] They also do no unrighteousness; they walk in His ways.
[4] You have ordained Your precepts, that we should keep them diligently.
[5] Oh that my ways may be established to keep Your statutes!
[6] Then I shall not be ashamed when I look upon all Your commandments.
[7] I shall give thanks to You with uprightness of heart, when I learn Your righteous judgments.
[8] I shall keep Your statutes; do not forsake me utterly!

1. List the words you found that refer to the Law (you should have seven).

Commandments

Strong's H4687 – *mitsvah*

1. the commandment (of God)

2. commandment (of code of wisdom {or conduct})

2. Who is being described in verses 1-3?

3. At what point does the psalmist shift his focus? What noticeable shift does he make?

4. Why do you think he shifted his focus? How can you apply that to your own focus?

5. What are the psalmist's feelings about God's law?

6. What benefits of God's word does he list?

7. Recalling what you have learned about the New Testament believer's relationship with the Mosaic laws, how can we live a life that is blameless?

Blameless H8549

1. sound, wholesome, unimpaired, innocent, having integrity
2. what is complete or entirely in accord with truth and fact

☐ *Read: Romans 9:30-33; Philippians 1:20; I Peter 4:15-16; I John 2:28-29*

8. From where does the ability to live our lives, without shame before God, come?

☐ **Read:** *Deuteronomy 31:6-8; Joshua 1:5-8; Hebrews 13:5-6*

9. What promises do we have from God?

10. What are the conditions of receiving those promises?

Forsake H5800

•*to leave, loose,*

•*to depart from,*

leave behind, leave,

let alone

•*to leave, abandon,*

•*to be deserted*

Many people hold fast to the promises written that God will, "...never leave us nor forsake us." That is a comforting promise indeed, yet it is not without responsibility on our part. This promise is not a "blank check" to sin freely and be comforted in knowing that God will never forsake us. Remember, on the cross, God forsook His only Son as he was cloaked with the totality of the sin of mankind, who consistently refused to walk in obedience to the laws and precepts ordained by God. *(Matthew 27:46)*

☐ **Read:** *Judges 16:20-21; I Samuel 16:14-15; Psalm 81:11-14; Romans 1:18-32*

11. What could cause God to forsake us?

12. Take a moment to imagine yourself in the sandals of Samson or King Saul. Describe what it feels like to be forsaken by God.

Diving Deeper- To learn more about Samson and Saul read Judges 16 and I Samuel 15. What caused God's spirit to depart from them?

13. Now, put yourself in Joshua's place *(Joshua 1:5-8)*. How does it feel to have a conditional promise from God that He will never fail or forsake you?

☐ *Read: John 15:1-11*

14. How can you ensure you will never know what is like to be forsaken?

DevArtio in a Nutshell

- [ ] Always begin with prayer. Ask the Lord to speak to you. Prepare your heart to receive the voice of the Lord. (John 10:27)

Record & Read

- [ ] Read the passage (silently or aloud) a few times.

- [ ] Circle the words/phrase that resonates with you.

- [ ] Write the words/phrase in the empty space.

Reflect

- [ ] Draw shapes, lines, shadings, etc...

- [ ] Focus on one word or the phrase and listen to Holy Spirit.

- [ ] Ask questions and wait for answers.

- [ ] Seek correction and guidance.....

Release & Respond

- [ ] Pray it all back to Abba and respond to His direction

Rest

- [ ] Bask in the quietness of your heart.

See chapter on creative prayer for more detailed instructions.

Psalm 119:1-3
1 How blessed are those whose way is blameless, who walk in the law of the Lord.
2 How blessed are those who observe His testimonies, who seek Him with all their heart.
3 They also do no unrighteousness; they walk in His ways.

¹ How blessed are those whose way is blameless, who walk in the law of the Lord.
² How blessed are those who observe His testimonies, who seek Him with all their heart.
³ They also do no unrighteousness; they walk in His ways.

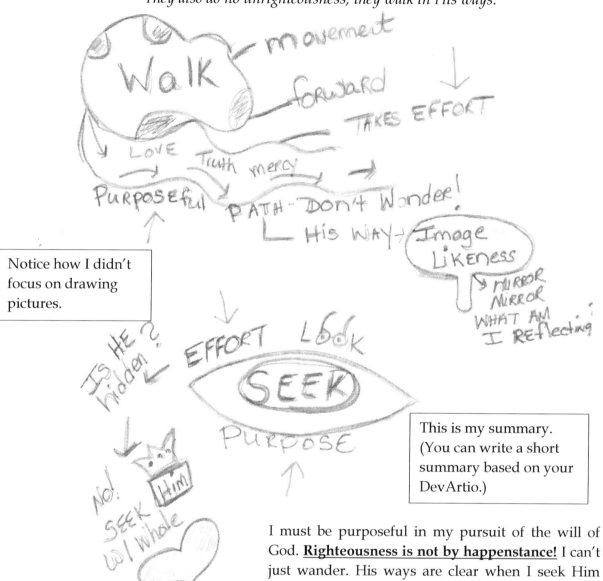

Notice how I didn't focus on drawing pictures.

This is my summary. (You can write a short summary based on your DevArtio.)

I must be purposeful in my pursuit of the will of God. **Righteousness is not by happenstance!** I can't just wander. His ways are clear when I seek Him with a sincere heart. My flesh will NEVER seek His ways! His testimonies are a witness to God. They show me His image and likeness. Know His word- know Him!

JOURNAL

As you consider your current walk with God and His word, are you able to say that your way is blameless? What would your blameless walk look like?

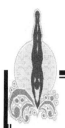

Diving Deeper

Being Forsaken

Use the blank space to write or draw your thoughts about this passage of scripture.

You can write from the perspective of Jesus or perhaps you'd like to choose an observer's viewpoint. What does being forsaken look like, feel like, smell like?

Think about those who were present. Imagine the onlookers, the Centurions, the disciples, or His mother, Mary. You may even want to look at it from the perspective of Heaven.

Can you imagine what God, His Father saw? What about the Angels?

Matthew 27:45-46

[45] Now from the sixth hour darkness fell upon all the land until the ninth hour. [46] About the ninth hour Jesus cried out with a loud voice, saying, "Eli, Eli, lama sabachthani?" that is, "My God, My God, why have You forsaken Me

Our Heavenly GPS System

Life as a military family was an adventure. It was a treat being able to visit many places that some could only read about in books. It was a joy having opportunities to enlarge our circle of friends with every relocation. Yet, for me, the one thing that cast a shadow on the excitement was the idea of driving around an unknown city or country, especially at night. That was never a pleasurable experience for me.

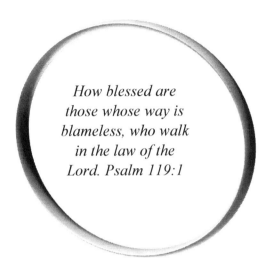

How blessed are those whose way is blameless, who walk in the law of the Lord. Psalm 119:1

I am self-diagnosed as "directionally challenged". I dislike being lost in unfamiliar territory to the point of breaking out in a sweat, increased heart rate and stomach pains during a "lost" moment. I am so thankful for the age of technology and access to on-line maps with directions. I will be forever grateful for the availability of the personal GPS system. No more panic attacks for me! Even when I miss a turn, that voice is there to guide me back onto the right path. It's not perfect, but is does ease many of my fears about being lost while navigating unknown paths.

I am even more thankful that, as children of The King, we also have access to a heavenly GPS. There are times in life when we travel in unfamiliar territories; we are unsure of what direction to take to arrive safely at our destination. We hesitate through the darkness because we can't see clearly. Yet, with "**G**od's **P**resence **S**ystem" we can be assured of accurate turn-by-turn instructions as we travel through life. Even if we happen to miss a turn, His voice, His word, and His Spirit, are all there to redirect us and get us back on the right path.

With our heavenly GPS we can choose to avoid roadblocks of unrighteousness. We can bypass the detours of doubt, fear, worry and anxiety. We can even program our favorite places to travel, such as: righteousness, peace, joy, love, grace...you name it and you can find directions to get there safely. Our job is to keep our GPS charged and updated. We charge up by continually plugging into His presence. We keep our GPS updated by plugging into and interfacing with God's word consistently.

God assures us that He will show us the path of life. He promises us that Holy Spirit will always be there to guide us. We can be confident of that still, small voice to whisper those "turn-by-turn" directions to us, as we travel through this life. When we keep our heavenly GPS in working condition, we will be able to navigate life's journey, even the darkest moments, with boldness, confidence and the assurance that comes from knowing our Father's voice, listening intently to His instructions, and faithfully following His "turn-by-turn" instructions.

We all have assigned destinies, and with our heavenly GPS we will be assured of a safe arrival. As you continue to study Psalm 119, think of God's laws, precepts, commands, ordinances, testimonies, words, judgments and ways, as a fail-safe GPS to keep you on the right path. If you ever feel that you are lost or have taken a wrong turn, never hesitate to stop and ask for direction(s) from His holy word. When we have faith in His promise that He will "...never leave us nor forsake us..." it gives us confidence to travel unknown paths knowing we have the best map and guidance system at our disposal. Knowing this enables us to take delight in the precious Law of the LORD!

Praying Psalm 119:1-8

Aleph א

Prayer Focus
The blessing of walking in obedience to the Law of the Lord

Ex: "*Father I bless you for Your wisdom that is contained in Your law, for I know that in Your words I find life and righteousness. Father, I thank you for Your wonderful law that is able to keep me pure. Forgive me for any transgression of Your word that has caused me to be defiled in any way...*"

1 How blessed are those whose way is blameless,
Who walk in the law of the Lord.
² How blessed are those who observe His testimonies,
Who seek Him with all *their* heart.
³ They also do no unrighteousness;
They walk in His ways.

> Read the next verse and offer a prayer based on the suggested Prayer Focus. If you are praying in a group, I suggest the facilitator guide the prayer time by reading the verse grouping and giving others time to verbalize a prayer. When you get a sense that everyone who wanted to pray has done so, move on the next verse group.

Prayer Focus
Walking in godly precepts will keep you unashamed before God

⁴ You have ordained Your precepts,
That we should keep *them* diligently.
⁵ Oh that my ways may be established
To keep Your statutes!
⁶ Then I shall not be ashamed
When I look upon all Your commandments.

⁷ I shall give thanks to You with uprightness of heart,
When I learn Your righteous judgments.
⁸ I shall keep Your statutes;
Do not forsake me utterly!

Prayer Focus
Praising God for His Everlasting presence

Creativity Page

Session Four

BETH

ב

Creativity Page

Review

- [ ] What is the basic purpose of Mosaic Law?

- [ ] How does it relate to New Testament believers?

- [ ] What does it mean to be blameless?

Getting Started

- [ ] When shopping, what is the difference when you are seeking a specific item versus when you are just browsing or wandering around for whatever catches your eye?

- [ ] What are the benefits and challenges to each method? Which one do you prefer?

Read Psalm 119: 9-16 — *Circle, highlight or underline the words that refer to God's law. Remember to record you findings in the law table located in the appendix.*

[9] How can a young man keep his way pure? By keeping it according to Your word.

[10] With all my heart I have sought You; do not let me wander from Your commandments.

[11] Your word I have treasured in my heart, that I may not sin against You.

[12] Blessed are You, O Lord; teach me Your statutes.

[13] With my lips I have told of all the ordinances of Your mouth.

[14] I have rejoiced in the way of Your testimonies, As much as in all riches.

[15] I will meditate on Your precepts and regard Your ways.

[16] I shall delight in Your statutes; I shall not forget Your word.

1. What question does the psalmist ask?

Read: Proverbs 20:9; Ecclesiastes 7:20; Isaiah 53:6; Romans 3:23; I John 1:8

2. Do you think it is possible to keep our ways pure (sinless)? Why or why not?

3. What is his answer to this question?

Insight on the Word

When translating the bible from Hebrew and Greek to English sometimes we miss the nuances of certain words. The word "word" in Psalm 119:9; John 15:3; John17:17; and Ephesians 5:25-27 is a good example.

Each of those words, *dabar* (H1697) in Psalm 119:5, *logos* (G3056) in John 15:3 and 17:17, and *rhema* (G4487) in Ephesians 5:25-27 denote more than just the written word. They refer to a spoken word, something that is uttered.

According to the Vine's Expository dictionary, the significance of *rhema* (as distinct from *logos*) is exemplified in the charge to take "the sword of the Spirit, which is the word of God", in Ephesians 6:17. Here the reference is not to the whole Bible, since it had not yet been printed as we know it today, but to the individual scripture which the Spirit brings to our remembrance for use in time of need, a prerequisite being the regular storing of the mind with Scripture *{to be spoken at the right time-Proverbs 25:11}*

Read: *John 15:3; 17:17; Ephesians 5:25-27*

4. How can the word of God keep us pure?

5. How intentional does the psalmist seem about seeking God? What actions does he take? Write your answer in the shape below.

*(The heart (H3820) refers to more than the organ that pumps blood. It is the center of everything we are, our feelings, will, and intellect. **www.blueletterbible.com**)*

6. Looking at Psalm 119:10-11, what doesn't the psalmist want to do?

7. Remember the shopping question from earlier? Compare shopping methods (intentional versus wandering) to the idea of intentionally seeking God's words, versus wandering from His commandments. Discuss the dangers and challenges of wandering compared to the benefits of seeking His direction intentionally. What mental image do you see when you think of a person wandering? Use the space below to write and/or draw your answer. (Remember, you do not have to be an artist to do this. Just draw what you see, using various shapes, lines, words, etc. Give yourself permission to take a leap of creative faith out of the familiar box of only writing your response).

Read: Psalm 119:21; Proverbs 21:16; 27:8;

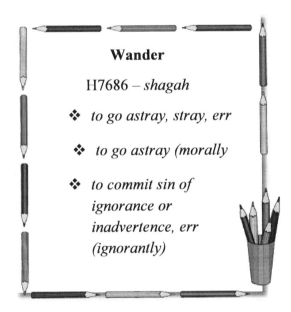

Wander

H7686 – *shagah*

❖ *to go astray, stray, err*

❖ *to go astray (morally*

❖ *to commit sin of ignorance or inadvertence, err (ignorantly)*

Read: *Deuteronomy 6:6; 11:18, 30:11-14; Psalm 37: 30,31; Jeremiah 31:33; Colossians 3:12-16*

8. What role does our heart play in keeping us aligned with the moral and social principles of God's word?

9. In Psalm 119:13-16, what are the verbs the psalmist uses to declare his relationship with God's word?

Read: *II Timothy 3:15-16*

10. Most people like a pleasant word from the Lord. What is your response when you come in contact with the spoken or written word of God in the various aspects of II Timothy 3:15-16?

Judgments/Ordinances

Strong's H4941 – mishpat

1. act of deciding a case
2. sentence, decision (of judgment)
3. execution (of judgment)
4. decision (in law)

"We might call this "case law". It's the verdicts or outcomes or formal decrees established based on resolving the situation brought before the court. It describes the practical application of the Law in situations not specifically detailed word for word so that we may understand how God's Word is applicable in every situation and that it provides no loopholes."

(Walk with the Word 1998-2010)

11. How can you be more intentional about delighting in all of the words and precepts of God?

DevArtJournal

DevArtio in a Nutshell

- ☐ Always begin with prayer. Ask the Lord to speak to you. Prepare your heart receive the voice of the Lord. (John 10:27)
- ☐ Do you remember your five "R" steps to DevArtio?

- ☐ Read the passage (silently or aloud) a few times

- ☐ Focus on the word "treasured" which means to hide, or store up.

- ☐ Draw or write your thoughts about what it means to treasure God's word in our hearts.

- ☐ What does that look like? What are benefits? How are you to accomplish that? What are the obstacles...?

- ☐ I suggest playing soft instrumental/"soaking" music in the background. Go to page 190 in the appendix to see a list of suggested music.

Psalm 119:11
11 Your word I have treasured in my heart, that I may not sin against You.

Creativity Page

JOURNAL

Does your walk with God resemble one that is intentional or one that is prone to wandering? What are some things that could cause you wander? What principles or precepts from God's word can you use to help keep you from wandering?

Praying Psalm 119:9-16

Beth בּ

Prayer Focus
The cleansing power
of God's Word

9 How can a young man keep his way pure?
By keeping *it* according to Your word.
10 With all my heart I have sought You;
Do not let me wander from
Your commandments.

Prayer Focus
The power of the
indwelling word of God

11 Your word I have treasured in my heart,
That I may not sin against You.
12 Blessed are You, O Lord;
Teach me Your statutes.

Prayer focus
Rejoicing in the righteous
ordinances (decisions) of the Lord

13 With my lips I have told of
All the ordinances of Your mouth.
14 I have rejoiced in the way of Your
testimonies, as much as in all riches.

Prayer Focus
Keeping
the Word of God in view

15 I will meditate on Your precepts
And regard Your ways.
16 I shall delight in Your statutes;
I shall not forget Your word.

Session Five

GIMEL

ג

Creativity Page

○ List the different words that refer to the law. (If you have color coded your words it will be easy to go back and find them).

Getting Started

○ Have you ever had your character slandered, been a victim of malicious gossip, or had others secretly undermine you at work, in your family or in ministry? How did you respond?

○ Did you seek out advice on how to handle the situation? From whom did you seek counsel?

○ Why are governmental laws (traffic, employment, civil, etc.) important to society? What would a society without governing laws look like?

Read: II Kings 6:15-17; Luke 8:10
Take a moment to ask God to open your eyes that you may see new and wondrous things from His law during this study.

Read: Psalm 119:17-24 – *Remember to color code your words, relating to the word law (law, statute, commandment, testimonies, precepts, judgments, word, ordinances).*

17 Deal bountifully with Your servant, that I may live and keep Your word.

18 Open my eyes, that I may behold Wonderful things from Your law.

19 I am a stranger in the earth; do not hide Your commandments from me.

20 My soul is crushed with longing after Your ordinances at all times.

21 You rebuke the arrogant, the cursed, who wander from Your commandments.

22 Take away reproach and contempt from me, for I observe Your testimonies.

23 Even though princes sit and talk against me, Your servant meditates on Your statutes.

24 Your testimonies also are my delight; they are my counselors, and I love them exceedingly.

1. When you think about all the laws and commandments in the bible, do you tend to think of them in terms of restrictions or in terms of gifts from God? Why?

2. What two requests does the psalmist ask of God in verses 17 and 18? Why?

Read: Leviticus 25:23; Psalm 24:1, 89:11, 115:16

3. Why would the psalmist consider himself to be a stranger?

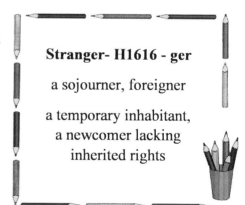

Stranger- H1616 - ger

a sojourner, foreigner

a temporary inhabitant, a newcomer lacking inherited rights

4. Why do foreigners need to know the laws of their host country?

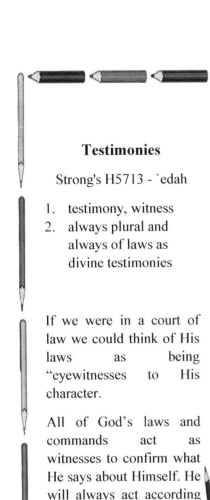

Testimonies

Strong's H5713 - `edah

1. testimony, witness
2. always plural and always of laws as divine testimonies

If we were in a court of law we could think of His laws as being "eyewitnesses to His character.

All of God's laws and commands act as witnesses to confirm what He says about Himself. He will always act according to His character which is corroborated by His laws.

Read: *Genesis 1:26-28; Numbers 15:16, Psalm 8:6; 115:16*

5. Why is it important for us to know the laws and precepts God has given to govern the Earth-our host country?

6. According to the psalmist, what kind of people wander? What is their fate?

7. In Psalm 119:23, who does he say was speaking against him?

Read: *Daniel 6:1-5*

8. The Hebrew word "princes" refer to the head person of any class with some sort of ruling or governmental authority, such as governors, captains, stewards, etc. Daniel had to contend with those in leadership positions who tried to manipulate him into acting contrary to law of his God. Have you ever faced a similar situation? What was your response?

9. Looking at Psalm 119:22-23, what do you think could have been the subject of their reproach against him?

10. What is the psalmist's response to being slandered?

11. What does he rely on for wise counsel?

Read: *I John 4:6; John 15:26-27; Proverbs 12:20*

12. Looking at the meaning of the word testimonies, how can they serve as our counselors?

Read: I Kings 12:1-14, 16-19, Exodus 18:14-27, II Chronicles 22:2-4; Proverbs 11:14, 12:20

13. What can be the benefits and risks of relying on human counselors? What qualities should we look for in human counselors before we take their advice? This a good place to make a list.

Benefits	Risks	Qualities

14. Think about a time when you have listened to or given "bad" counsel. What would you do differently?

DevArtJournal

Psalm 119:23-24
[23] Even though princes sit and talk against me, Your servant meditates on Your statutes.
[24] Your testimonies also are my delight; they are my counselors. And I love them exceedingly.

DevArtio

As you proceed with this week's DevArtio assignment, think about a major conflict you have encountered or perhaps one you foresee in the near future. What could you have done differently? How can this week's lesson help you navigate conflict with confidence and integrity?

Draw your answer here or use your journal to discuss your answer.

What changes do you need to make in regards to responding to conflict or dealing with those who unfairly speak against you or who you know are purposely seeking to do you harm?

How refreshing to see our Father's laws, commandments, and statutes with new eyes! How liberating it is to relinquish the view of them as burdens and chains to keep us fearfully obedient to a strict master! How wonderful to bask in the joy and privilege of receiving the gift of a personal counselor to guide us through life! This counselor is Holy Spirit, of Whom Jesus says ,"But when He, the Spirit of truth, comes, He will guide you into all the truth" (John 16:13). While it is wise to seek counsel from others when in need, we must be wise and discerning and ensure that those we seek counsel from are also seeking counsel in the word of God and by the Spirit of God.

Praying Psalm 119:17-24

Gimel ג

Prayer Focus
The revelatory power of God's word

¹⁷ Deal bountifully with Your servant, That I may live and keep Your word.
¹⁸ Open my eyes, that I may behold Wonderful things from Your law

Prayer Focus
Desire and longing for direction found in the Word.

¹⁹ I am a stranger in the earth; Do not hide Your commandments from me.
²⁰ My soul is crushed with longing After Your ordinances at all times.

Prayer Focus
The Word of God as your counselor in time of distress or conflict

²¹ You rebuke the arrogant, the cursed, Who wander from Your commandments.
²² Take away reproach and contempt from me, For I observe Your testimonies.
²³ Even though princes sit and talk against me, Your servant meditates on Your statutes.
²⁴ Your testimonies also are my delight; They are my counselors and I love them exceedingly.

Session Six

DALETH

ד

Creativity Page

Review

☐ What is the meaning of the word testimonies?

Getting Started

☐ Think about one of the lowest points in your life. What were the circumstances and how did you make it through that time?

☐ How do you respond when you realize your actions or choices are the source of trouble in your life?

☐ Have you ever trusted or vouched for someone and ended up disappointed or embarrassed? What was your relationship with that person afterwards?

Read Psalm 119:25-32 – *don't forget to color code your words.*

25 My soul cleaves to the dust; revive me according to Your word.
26 I have told of my ways, and You have answered me; teach me Your statutes.
27 Make me understand the way of Your precepts, so I will meditate on Your wonders.
28 My soul weeps because of grief; strengthen me according to Your word.
29 Remove the false way from me, and graciously grant me Your law.
30 I have chosen the faithful way; I have placed Your ordinances before me.
31 I cling to Your testimonies; O LORD, do not put me to shame!
32 I shall run the way of Your commandments, for You will enlarge my heart.

1. How would you describe the emotional state of the psalmist at the beginning of this stanza?

Read: *Joshua 7:1-6; Isaiah 47:1; Job 7:20-21; Psalm 113:7-8*

2. What does dust symbolize?

3. What does he ask God to do in Psalm 119: 25, 28?

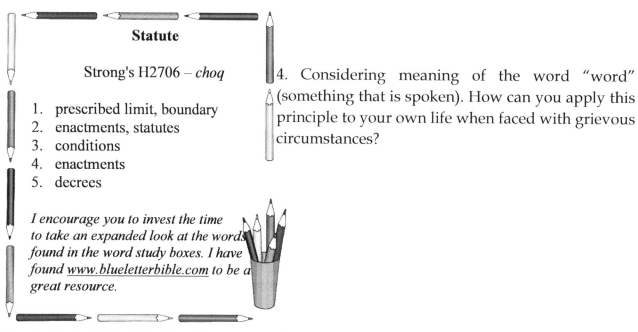

Statute

Strong's H2706 – *choq*

1. prescribed limit, boundary
2. enactments, statutes
3. conditions
4. enactments
5. decrees

I encourage you to invest the time to take an expanded look at the words found in the word study boxes. I have found www.blueletterbible.com to be a great resource.

4. Considering meaning of the word "word" (something that is spoken). How can you apply this principle to your own life when faced with grievous circumstances?

Read: *Psalm 37:5-6; II Chronicles 7:14; Psalm 51; I John 1:9*

5. Looking at Psalm 119:26-27 and the above verses, what is the source of the psalmist's troubles? What is his solution?

6. In Psalm 119:29-32 the psalmist makes a choice. What is that choice and why is it necessary in the life of a believer?

7. What insight have you gained about the possible source of his grief?

8. Where does he place the responsibility for the source of his grief and what example does that set for us?

9. What assurance does the psalmist ask for in return for his obedience?

Read: Psalm 25:20-22; Jeremiah 29:10-14; Joel 2:25-27; Philippians 1:19-20

10. How can we be assured that we will not be put to shame?

11. Compare the psalmist's condition in verse 32 to his condition in verse 25 in Psalm 119.

12. To what do you attribute this change and how can you apply this during your times of grief or stress?

13. What final resolution does the psalmist make in verse 32?

14. . How can he be assured of success?

15. How does the physical condition of your heart affect your endurance when engaging in exercise?

Read: *Deuteronomy 11:18; II Kings 23:24-25; Ps 37:31, Jeremiah 31:33; I Corinthians 9:24-25; Hebrews 12:1; I Timothy 4:7-8*

16. How does the spiritual condition of your heart affect your ability to run the race of obedience with endurance?

DevArtJournal

Heart Monitor (Spiritual EKG)

Instructions-(there is an example on the next page and a blank form on the following page)

Heart Moved

−   +

1	2	3	4	5	VS	Observation
					25	o **Read** each verse. Place a dot on the graph next to verse number indicating how the verse impacts you.
					26	o **Connect** the dots so you have a graph line. This will show you at glance which verses impacted you most.
					27	o **Record** your observations. Explain why/how the verses impacted you. Note how the verse challenged, encouraged or convicted you. You may not have a comment for every verse. That is fine.
					28	
					29	o You can incorporate this method during your future quiet times using any passage of scripture.
					30	
					31	o There is a blank form in the appendix that you may use to make copies or go to www.swatbookcamp.com to request a copy in a word document.
					32	

Prescription (what are you going to do?):

o   Write your prescription. Ask God to show you at least one application to your life.

o   If it is not too personal, share it with someone.

Adapted from *Learn to Study the Bible* (Deane 2009)

Heart Moved

− +

1	2	3	4	5	VS	Observation
					21	(21) This verse convicted me because there was a time when I was deep in debt and hiding from creditors. I considered bankruptcy. This verse exhorted me to walk in integrity with my finances. I wanted to be generous but debt prevented me.
					22	(vs.23)I know when I follow God's way He will take delight in that because He delights in Himself for He said of all that he creates "it is good".
					23	
					24	(vs. 24) This reminded me that I will have times of "falling" but I will never be utterly destroyed. He is there to catch me. I imagine a child tripping over something while holding hand and walking with a parent. The parent will not the child fall as long as his hands are being held. It's when the child lets go that they completely fall. I will keep my hand in God's hand! Because I am "clumsy" (prone to sin).
					25	
					26	(vs 25) In times of worry about a need (usually financial) this verses sustained me. I was assured that as long as pursued righteousness I would have my needs met. (Matt. 6:33)

(vs 26) It is my goal to be gracious to others who are in need and teach my children and grandchildren to do the same. |

Prescription (what are you going to do?) I vowed to walk in integrity with my finances and pursue freedom from debt by paying what I owe. NO excuses. I now advise others to do the same. While I understand that God can cause favor to come to me and erase or decrease my debt, my responsibility is to PAY what I OWE. I stopped worrying about having enough and started concerning myself with the needs of others. God has been true to His word. I have NEVER been in want or need of anything of importance. I am pleased to testify that after years being in debt to tune of hundreds of thousands of dollars (mostly credit card debt) we (my husband and I) are within 18 months of freedom!

YOUR TURN...

Heart Moved

-				+		
1	**2**	**3**	**4**	**5**	**VS**	*Observation*
					25	
					26	
					27	
					28	
					29	
					30	
					31	
					32	

Prescription (what are you going to do?):

Proverbs 23:19

Listen, my son, and be wise, and direct your heart in the way.

Psalm 119:32

I shall run the way of Your commandments, for You will enlarge my heart.

In what matters do you need to be more diligent conditioning your heart to run the race with delight and obedience?

Prescription for Joy

In the beginning of this stanza it is obvious the psalmist was experiencing deep grief or affliction and needed encouragement. He knew he could find what he needed in God's word. Remember, the meaning for "word" in this instance is that which is spoken. There is something powerful about speaking God's over your situation. The Bible tells us death and life are in the power of the tongue (Proverbs 18:21). The prescription for your sorrow and grief is found in the power of the word of God and on your lips.

Just as David encouraged himself in the Lord and asked for ephod (which was a method for hearing God speak) after the Amalekites had attacked his people and stolen their families and possessions, we must know how to speak the word of God over our situations that try rob us of our joy. We have been given access to the joy of the Lord which cannot be taken away (*John 17:13-14; John 16:22-24*). We are citizens of the Kingdom of God and joy is a benefit and by-product of our citizenship. (*Romans 14:17; Galatians 5:22*)

In order to maintain our joy, confession and repentance must be a consistent habit in our lifestyle. We must acknowledge our failures and intentionally leave our way of sin and follow God's ways. That is true repentance. When we choose to operate by godly principles of righteousness, we can see wonders of God at work in our personal life, our homes, our jobs, and our ministries.

Trying to live the way of the world, instead of the Word, will cause us grief. We cannot operate in falseness and in the truth of God's word at the same time. Truth cannot co-exist with a lie. We cannot live double lives. As you can see from reading this stanza, straying from God's commands, precepts, and statutes can cause grief and sorrow. He has ordained paths of truth for us to journey on through our time here on Earth.

I encourage you to follow the example of King Solomon and ask God to enlarge your heart with wisdom that you may follow His ways *(I Kings 3:9; 4:29)*. Be quick to acknowledge your sins, repent and seek reconciliation with God that you may be revived and refreshed *(Acts 3:19)*. When you make an intentional decision to live for God, and be obedient to His word, you will not be put to shame on Earth or Heaven. Glory be to God!

Praying Psalm 119:25-32

Daleth 7

Prayer Focus
The reviving power of God's word

25 My soul cleaves to the dust; Revive me according to Your word.
26 I have told of my ways, and You have answered me; Teach me Your statutes.
27 Make me understand the way of Your precepts, So I will meditate on Your wonders.
28 My soul weeps because of grief; Strengthen me according to Your word.

Prayer Focus
Walking faithfully in the truth of the Word

29 Remove the false way from me, And graciously grant me Your law.
30 I have chosen the faithful way; I have placed Your ordinances before me.

Prayer Focus
For God to fill your heart with His wisdom

31 I cling to Your testimonies; O LORD, do not put me to shame!
32 I shall run the way of Your commandments, For You will enlarge my heart.

Session Seven

HE

ה

Creativity Page

Review

☐ What is the meaning of the word statute?

Getting Started

☐ Have you ever participated in any kind of choreographed group dance? (This can include line dances). What was the most difficult thing for you during this activity?

☐ What would you say is the most important quality to have to be successful at line dancing? Why?

Read Psalm 119:33-40

[33] Teach me, O LORD, the way of Your statutes, and I shall observe it to the end.

[34] Give me understanding, that I may observe Your law and keep it with all my heart.

[35] Make me walk in the path of Your commandments, for I delight in it.

[36] Incline my heart to Your testimonies and not to dishonest gain.

[37] Turn away my eyes from looking at vanity, and revive me in Your ways.

[38] Establish Your word to Your servant, as that which produces reverence for You.

[39] Turn away my reproach which I dread, for Your ordinances are good.

[40] Behold, I long for Your precepts; revive me through Your righteousness.

Read: *Psalm 119:102; Proverbs 4:10-12; Deuteronomy 6:3-5; James. 1:5; I Samuel 12:24*

1. Discuss the concept of reciprocity (mutual exchange) as it relates to Psalm 119:33-34. Why is this important?

Read: *II Kings 23:24-25; Matthew 22:36-40; James 1:22-25*

2. Explain the importance of the relationship between the heart and mind, as it relates to your willingness to be obedient to the things of God.

3. Name three parts of the body, that the psalmist offers up to God, in his quest to honor the LORD with obedience in Psalm 119: 33-40.

4. Think about the line dancing question in the Getting Started section. How important is unity and alignment in regards to choreography and dancing in step with other?

Read: *Isaiah 33:13-16*

5. Why is having your whole body in alignment an important aspect of your relationship with God and His word?

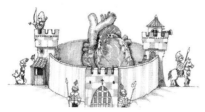

dunehypnotherapy.co.uk

Read: *Psalm 141:4; Proverbs 4:20-23; I Timothy 6:10*

5. Why must we guard our heart's inclinations? What is the danger of not guarding our hearts?

Read: *Psalm 16:11, 23:3; Proverbs 4:18; Isaiah 26:7-8*

6. What are the results of having this type of synergy in your body when it comes to following the paths LORD?

7. The psalmist makes many requests in this stanza. What are his requests in Psalm 119:38-39?

Read: *Exodus 20:6, 23:22; Psalm 112:1, 128:1; Luke 11:28*

8. We know God will keep his promises to His people without fail. What are the conditions to His promises?

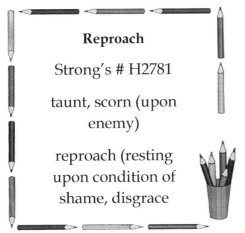

Reproach

Strong's # H2781

taunt, scorn (upon enemy)

reproach (resting upon condition of shame, disgrace

9. In Psalm 119:39, the psalmist writes about being reproached. Looking at the definition of the word reproach and the context of this stanza, what type of reproach do you think the psalmist dreading and from whom?

10. How did that affect the psalmist?

Read: *Psalm 39:8; 69: 5-13; 89:50-52*

12. What further insight do you get from these verses?

12. What was the psalmist's conclusion about the validity of God's ordinances?

13. Have you or do you experience being mocked for your faith? How did/do you respond?

14. Has there been a time in your life when your sins where known by others and you experienced reproach from non-believers? A common example is "I thought you were saved. How could you...?" What are some things people said to you? How did it make you feel? How did you respond?

Read: *Luke 6:22-23; I Peter 4:14-18; I John 1:9*
15. What promises can you stand upon during these times?

16. Have you ever mocked a person or group for their adherence to their faith that is different than yours? If so, what was your basis for mocking (reproach)? What is an appropriate alternative?

Read: *Psalm 119:40; II Chronicles 15:3-4; Jeremiah 29:11-13; Luke 6:21; I Peter. 2:2*

17. When we set our desires to know God's heart and seek Him through His word what can we expect?

16. Look at the image on this page. How can you connect it to Psalm 119:40?

DevArtJournal

Turn away my eyes from looking at vanity, and revive me in Your ways.

DevArtio

In Psalm 119:18, you focused on asking God to open your eyes that you may see wondrous things from His law. Now, I want you to focus on things you should be turning your eyes away from in order to see His beauty more clearly.

Read the verse as many times as needed until a key word or phrase impacts you. Write them down and begin to meditate (with color of course) and ask God to speak to you and show you what He has to say to you concerning this verse.

Do you remember the five steps of DevArtio?

Go to page six for more in depth explanation of DevArtio process

Psalm 119:37
Turn away my eyes from looking at vanity, and revive me in Your ways.

You can use this space to summarize your DevArtio session, write a prayer, or journal your thoughts about the above verse.

It Takes All of You

Teach me, O Lord, the way of Your statutes, And I shall observe it to the end, says the psalmist in Psalm 119:33. The word "teach" in Hebrew is "yara". Some of its meanings are: to point out, inform, to direct, or to shoot as an arrow. Just as an arrow should follow the course the archer has planned as he released it from the bow, when I choose to be obedient I am like a well-pointed arrow in the hands of God.

When an archer releases the arrow he knows that it will take the combined energy and effort of his eyes, arms, shoulders, and other parts of his body along with proper breathing techniques, to ensure the arrow will reach its intended target. Just as the archer and the arrow are depending on the unity of the archer's body, connecting with God takes the partnership of mind, heart, and body. We must seek to have an understanding of God's word with our minds to be able to hide or treasure it in our hearts. In turn, what we know in our minds and believe in hearts will govern our body and we can submit ourselves wholly to the word of God with joy and conviction and not out of compulsion. We must be willing to offer our whole bodies as living sacrifices unto our God. Unlike the animals, who were sacrificed without choice or voice, we have the ability to choose to offer ourselves up to holiness and righteousness. The animals only hope after sacrifice was death yet as we willingly submit ourselves to God's commands, our post-sacrificial hope is walking in the fullness of joy on this earth (Psalm 16:11) eternal life after physical death. These are promises God has given to those who keep His word. **When our prayers are coupled with obedience we can be assured that God will keep His promises.**

What He doesn't promise is that the wait to see those prayers manifested will be free of obstacles. Sometimes that wait, and our steadfast faith, will cause us to be the object of derision among non-believers and sometime even those who believe. Even though no one likes being mocked, when the mocking is because of our love and obedience to God's word, we can endure it knowing that we are producing righteousness (I Peter 4:14). The key is not to faint in the waiting process (II Corinthians 4:16-17; Hebrews 12:1-4). Do not to turn from the word of God just to appease the mockers. Wait on the Lord and be of good courage! Stay on the path He has directed; for it is a good path and it is the chosen path that leads to life.

Continue to seek His word as a newborn babe seeks milk for nourishment. Our longing for hearing God speak through His word should be akin to a deep hunger or thirst. If we go without it, we will feel weak, parched and in need of nourishment from the Lord. His word will revive us and refresh us during those dry seasons. His joy will be our strength. Take delight in that, my friend!

Praying Psalm 119:33-40

HE ה

As we have discussed the importance of aligning our whole being with the truth of God's word, I want you to add a new element to your prayer this week. As you pray the verses, I want you to touch or to move the body part involved in that particular verse. If the verse talks about the eyes, touch your eyes while praying. If the verse talks about walking, you can walk in place while praying. Some verses may not mention a body part specifically, so it will be left up to your discretion what to do in that instance. This is a wonderful way to stay engaged during prayer, and to remind yourself that it will take the partnership of your entire being to remain faithful to precepts of our God.

Prayer Focus
The ability to understand God's word with your mind and your heart

> 33 Teach me, O Lord, the way of Your statutes, And I shall observe it to the end.
> 34 Give me understanding, that I may observe Your law And keep it with all my heart

Prayer Focus
Submission of whole being to the truth of God's word

> 35 Make me walk in the path of Your commandments, For I delight in it.
> 36 Incline my heart to Your testimonies And not to dishonest gain.
> 37 Turn away my eyes from looking at vanity, And revive me in Your ways.

Prayer Focus
Promises kept to those who remain faithful to God's ordinances

> 38 Establish Your word to Your servant, As that which produces reverence for You.
> 39 Turn away my reproach, which I dread, For Your ordinances are good.

Prayer Focus
Desire for personal or corporate revival

> 40 Behold, I long for Your precepts; Revive me through Your righteousness.

91

Psalm 119:37 by Monica Allen

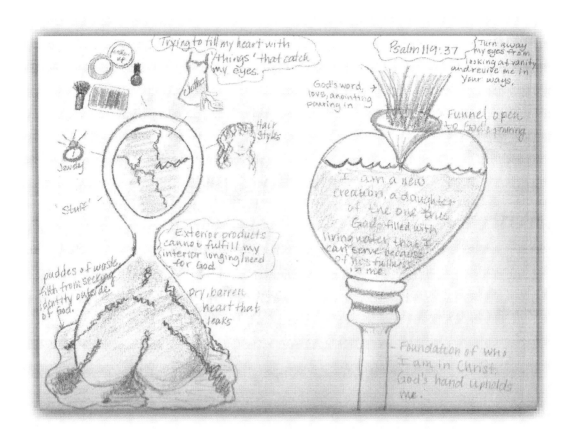

SESSION EIGHT

VAV

ו

Creativity Page

Review

☐ What is the meaning of the word heart?

☐ Why does it need to be guarded?

Getting Started

☐ Discuss a time when you purchased a product or service based on the advertisement and ended up disappointed? What was the product? Why were you disappointed?

☐ Discuss the importance of someone keeping their promises. How do you feel when others break promises made to you or someone else? Why?

◻ What do you think of when you hear the word "rules" or "boundaries"?

Read Psalm 119: 41-48

41 May Your loving kindnesses also come to me, O LORD, Your salvation according to Your word;

42 So I will have an answer for him who reproaches me, For I trust in Your word.

43 And do not take the word of truth utterly out of my mouth, for I wait for Your ordinances.

44 So I will keep Your law continually, Forever and ever.

45 And I will walk at liberty, for I seek Your precepts.

46 I will also speak of Your testimonies before kings and shall not be ashamed.

47 I shall delight in Your commandments, which I love.

48 And I shall lift up my hands to Your commandments, which I love; and I will meditate on Your statutes.

Precepts

Strong's H6490 – *piqquwd*

precept, statute

It is translated as statute 2x and commandment 2x in the KJV.

Webster's

1. Any commandment, instruction, order or direction given as a an authoritative rule of action or conduct;

2. a maxim (general truth), a restriction as to moral conduct;

3. a procedural directive or rule; Law: written order issued pursuant to law

In other words, precepts teach us how we are to govern ourselves based on the written law. For example, the Law states *"Honor your father and your mother, that your days may be prolonged in the land which the LORD your God gives you." Exodus 20:12.*

That means the principles that guide our actions, speech, and our counsel to others should fall in line with the idea of honoring our parents. Cursing, maltreatment, or disobedience violates the principle of the Law. This can explain why the precept (a rule of action based on written law) of stoning unto death was the consequence of a disobedient child in the Old Testament. (*Exodus 21:15; Leviticus 20:9; Deuteronomy 21:18-21; Proverbs 20:20*). Disobedience to a parent could cut one's life short.

We are to live our lives guided by precepts based on the Spirit of the Law. God still wants us to honor our parents because His character of honor has not changed. The punitive consequences (stoning to death) was taken care of on Calvary through the sacrifice of Jesus Christ. I know quite a few children who should shout hallelujah for that!!!

1. What does the psalmist desire in verse 119:41-43? Why?

Read: Psalm 37:39-40; 40:9-13; 71:10-13

2. In regards to salvation, what do you think the writer is referring to in Psalm 119:41?

Read: I Kings 8:56; Joshua 21:45, 23:14; Psalm 105:8-9, 42-43;

3. On what does the psalmist base his assurance that God will act according to His word?

Read: Luke 24:49; Acts 1:4-5; 13:32-33, 38-39; Galatians 3:13-14, 26-29; Romans 9:6-8; I John 2:23-25

4. According to the above verses, what promises do we have? What are the conditions to those promises? This is a good place to make a list.

Promises	Conditions

How wonderful it is to know we count on our Father to keep His promises!

The psalmist frequently asks for God to help him respond to those who reproach and taunt him for his steadfastness and belief in God. During the psalmist's time, there were various cultures who espoused beliefs in hundreds of different gods. Those who remained faithful to the LORD, and lived their lives according to His commands, in spite of hardships, were a stark contrast to those indulged in idol worship and the activities that came with it. Things such as human sacrifice, orgies as a means of worship, and other rituals that were contrary to the holy nature of the one true God, were the norm.

It is not much different for us today. We are bombarded daily with the idea of "eat, drink, and be merry", you only live once, and other ideas of self-pleasure, without the need of rules or boundaries. The freedom to live our belief without persecution (physical, verbal, governmental) is being tested daily. The psalmist was expressing his frustration with time and culture in which he lived. He wanted to be able to speak truth to the masses who reproached him. Just like the psalmist we should always be prepared to give an answer to the source of our hope. The word of truth should always be in our mouth. In this day of advanced technology and social media, we have a plethora of ways to engage the masses in truthful dialogue. Do you feel you are equipped to answer those who reproach you?

Read: Matthew 10:19-20; Luke 21:10-15; II Timothy 4:13-16; I Peter 3:13-17

5. What is the basis for our confidence in responding to those who reproach us for our belief?

Liberty

Strong's H7342 – *rachab*

1. broad, wide

Let's take a look at the source of our ability to speak and live boldly before others and God.

Read: Proverbs 4:10-12; John 8:31-32, 36; II Corinthians 3:15-17; Galatians 5:1, 13-14; James 1:25; I Peter 2:16

6. Some people equate rules and boundaries with a lack or loss of freedom. In Psalm 119:45-47, the psalmist links delighting in and following godly precepts to walking in liberty and not being ashamed before kings. How can rules and boundaries equate to freedom and boldness?

DevArtio

Imagine being put into an unfamiliar and expansive forest. You are then told there are various animals, reptiles, bugs and other indigenous inhabitants in that forest with you but you are not told where they are located. How much of the forest would you be willing to explore?

Now imagine you have been told exactly where those animals, bugs, and reptiles are located and were given a map of the forest with their location. How much of the forest would you be willing to explore with the map in hand?

Use this space to write or draw your response to the following phrase:

"Boundaries breed boldness."

Do you agree or disagree? Why?

Psalm 119:45

And I will walk at liberty, for I seek Your precepts.

Psalm 119:46

I will also speak of Your testimonies before kings and shall not be ashamed.

What can keep you from speaking the word of truth before others? Do you struggle with fear, shame, lack of knowledge, or your own disobedience? What steps do you need to take to address those issues?

That's Good News

We can trust God to keep his promises. We must first know what those promises are before we can rest in them. Knowing what God has already said can help us during the times we need rescue from a situation, or a person that is causing distress. God reminds us that His word will not return void. It will accomplish all that He set it out to do. He challenges us to prove Him faithful to His promises. If we can find it so easy to believe in the myriad of advertisements that claim to improve us from head to toe, and we know they benefit financially from our faith in them, then why can't we just take God at His word, knowing He isn't the one who reaps the benefits? Yet, just as with those infomercials, we must heed the fine print in God's words. Walking in obedience to His law, by the Spirit, gives us the spiritual, moral and emotional freedom to claim the truths spoken in His Word.

When we live by faith and obedience, we can speak the truth with power and boldness. Once again, if we heed the fine print, we see we must abide in Christ and His Spirit must abide in us, to be able to guide our mouths in right speech. We must speak only what He has spoken to us, either through the written word or through the voice of Holy Spirit. When we stick with speaking what was already spoken by God, we can be confident in speaking godly truth before anyone. When we live by godly precepts, we have the freedom to recognize boundaries and to make wise choices in alignment with the will of God.

Creative Challenge: Design a billboard advertisement describing the benefits of living by faith and obedience.

*Ex. **If you live in alignment, you can walk boldly in your assignment!***

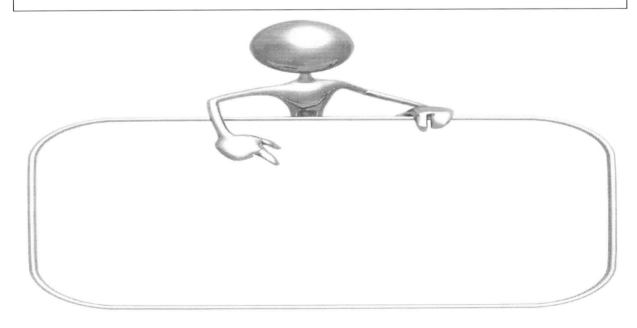

PRAYING PSALM 119:41-49
VAV ו

Prayer Focus
Hope and confidence in
God's Word

⁴¹ May Your loving kindnesses also come to me, O LORD, Your salvation according to Your word;
⁴² So I will have an answer for him who reproaches me, For I trust in Your word.
⁴³ And do not take the word of truth utterly out of my mouth, For I wait for Your ordinances.

Prayer Focus
Freedom found in seeking and
keeping God's commands

⁴⁴ So I will keep Your law continually, Forever and ever.
⁴⁵ And I will walk at liberty, For I seek Your precepts.

Prayer focus
Boldness in witnessing to others

⁴⁶ I will also speak of Your testimonies before kings And shall not be ashamed.

Prayer Focus
Delighting in the law of the LORD

⁴⁷ I shall delight in Your commandments, Which I love.
⁴⁸ And I shall lift up my hands to Your commandments, Which I love; And I will meditate on Your statutes.

Creativity Page

SESSION NINE

ZAYIN

ז

Creativity Page

Word Study Review

Time for a quick review. Match the word on the left with its definition on the right. (The answer key is located at the bottom of this page). Try rereading the first nine verses of Psalm 119 and inserting the definitions in place of the actual words. We still have one more word to add to the list. Can you figure out the missing word? Check your Law Table in the appendix to help you discover the missing word.

1. Law	A. direction given to teach us how we are to govern ourselves based on the written law
2. Commandment	B. something that is uttered
3. Testimonies	C. system of principles or instruction; legal directives
4. Precepts	
5. Statutes	D. prescribed limit, boundary
6. Ordinances/Judgments	E. a witness
	F. describes the practical application of the law
7. Word	G. code of wisdom or conduct

Answer Key

1-C; 2-G; 3-E; 4-A; 5-D; 6-F; 7-B

How did you do on the review? Hopefully you were able to remember most of them. Sometimes it helps to rewrite definitions in your own words to aid in memorization. Shall we continue? Do you have your colored pens and pencils handy? What about that steaming cup of coffee or tea? Let's begin!

Getting Started

- ☐ What do you see in society that angers or grieves you? Why does it anger or grieve you?

- ☐ What is your response or your solution?

Read Psalm 119:49-56. -*Remember to record your notes about the words that refer to law in the law table in the appendix.*

⁴⁹ Remember the word to Your servant, in which You have made me hope.
⁵⁰ This is my comfort in my affliction, that Your word has revived me.
⁵¹ The arrogant utterly deride me, yet I do not turn aside from Your law.
⁵² I have remembered Your ordinances from of old, O LORD, and comfort myself.
⁵³ Burning indignation has seized me because of the wicked, who forsake Your law.
⁵⁴ Your statutes are my songs in the house of my pilgrimage.
⁵⁵ O LORD, I remember Your name in the night, and keep Your law.
⁵⁶ This has become mine, that I observe Your precepts.

1. What is the overall theme of this stanza?

2. How would you describe the mood of the psalmist?

3. What is the source of his affliction?

4. Where does the psalmist find comfort?

Read: *Romans 15:4; II Timothy 3:16*

5. How do the above passages relate to Psalm 119:49-56?

Read: Psalm 42:3, 10; 69:9-13; 123:4; Luke 23:34-39

6. In Psalm119:51 the psalmist talks about facing derision from the arrogant. What are some of the reasons believers experienced mocking or ridicule?

7. What kind of people were the source of their derision?

8. What are some reasons that we may face ridicule or derision? From what kind of people can we expect this kind of behavior?

9. What do you think is the goal of those who ridicule and attack Christians for their beliefs? Can you list some examples?

In Psalm 119:53, the psalmist talks about his "burning indignation". In the KJV the phrase is translated as the word "horror". It means to have a burning, raging heat.

10. Who is this rage directed against?

11. Looking the meaning of the word forsake. Discuss why he should he be angry at those people.

FORSAKE

STRONG'S H5800 - `AZAB

to leave
to depart from
leave behind
abandon
forsake
neglect
apostatize

Read Hebrews 6:4-8 and discuss the danger of forsaking the truth.

12. What is his response to his anger?

13. What causes you to have burning indignation? What is your response?

As believers, we will have many reasons to be righteously angry about something or even with someone. Our job is use wisdom and discernment when responding to those situations or people. Let's take a look at how Nehemiah and Jesus responded when experiencing burning indignation at those who had forsaken the Law of the LORD.

Read: *Psalm 69:9; Nehemiah 13:7-11, 17, 25; John 2:13-17*

14. Who was angry in these verse? Why were they angry? Who was the object of their anger? What action did they take? (This is good place to make a comparison chart to keep your answers organized).

Who was angry?	At whom were they angry and why?	What was the response?

15. Summarize your comparison chart.

Let's take a further look at responding to anger.

Read: *Ephesians 4:26-27; Psalm 8-11*

16. What do these verses say about responding to our anger?

17. What is your conclusion, based on what you have just read, regarding righteous anger?

Creative Challenge (optional)

Draw a visual representation of your burning indignation

---

18. What are some examples of people or issues that we, as followers of Christ should be angry about? What is a solution for our response?

19. Can you think of any modern-day examples of righteous indignation being taken too far?

20. What is the psalmist's overall response experiencing mocking from the arrogant and burning indignation toward those who forsake the Law of the LORD?

21. How does seeing his response help you to deal with your feelings about those who mock you or other believers?

22. What does the psalmist say about songs?

Read: Isaiah 30:29; Job 35:10; Psalm 42:8; Acts 16:25-26

23. There is a recurring theme about songs in the night. What does the night represent and what is the power and purpose of a song during that time?

Praise Break

List five of your favorite songs or hymns. Why are these your favorite?

1.

2.

3.

4.

5.

Take a break and listen to a few of your favorites while thinking about the reasons why they are your favorites. Perhaps you will fall in love with them in new way.

DevArtJournal

Your statutes are my songs in the house of my pilgrimage.

In the space below practice writing a psalm by rewriting Psalm 119:49-56 using your own words. On the following journal page you will be writing your own psalm.

The Power of a Song

Some people call the book of Psalms the songbook of the Bible. Indeed, many of the Psalms have musical instructions included.

The writers used psalms or songs to give voice to their emotions, lament their situations, express joy, cry out to God for help or even sometimes to wish harm upon their enemies. Their songs were an honest and fully transparent view into their innermost thoughts and feelings.

Generally the psalms contain a similar format:

A. God is addressed

B. A problem is presented to Him

C. A statement of God's power over the problem

D. A statement of trust in Him to handle the problem

E. A plea for His help or intervention

F. A statement of faith that the problem is taken care of by God.

G. Close with a praise to God

Use this space to write your own psalm. Decide on the subject: praise, lament, cry for help, anger, repentance, a problem, etc…
I suggest playing some instrumental music in the background while you write your psalm.

The ABCs of a Psalm

A. God is addressed

B. A problem is presented to Him

C. A statement of God's power over the problem

D. Your trust in Him to handle the problem

E. A plea for His help or intervention

F. A statement of faith that is taken care of

G. Close with a praise to God

(You do not have to include every element. This is your psalm.)

STANDING FIRM

Just like the psalmist, there may be times when we cry out in distress for God to remember His promises to us. It is during those times of distress, pain, anxiety, fear, worry, doubt or confusion that we must remember the word of God which is given to us for instruction and encouragement. Yet, before we can remember these word we must first know them. That is why a consistent time of reading and praying God's word is necessary for a believer. Knowing

God's word, and knowing the standard He has set forth in His word, will give us the confidence, courage and boldness to stand firm.

We may face scorn, ridicule, harassment and mocking from those who stand proudly against God but we must stand firm. In the face of the blurred lines of cultural norms, we are obligated, as the psalmist was, not to turn aside from the Law of the LORD.

Some examples of this happening are evident in recent news.

> *"American fast-food chain Chick-fil-A was the focus of controversy following a series of public comments made in June 2012 by chief operating officer Dan Cathy opposing same-sex marriage. This followed reports that Chick-fil-A's charitable endeavor, the S. Truett Cathy-family-operated WinShape Foundation, had made millions in donations to political organizations which oppose LGBT rights. LGBT rights activists called for protests and boycotts of the chain, while counter-protestors rallied in support by eating at the restaurants. National political figures both for and against the actions spoke out and some business partners severed ties with the chain. In March 2014, tax filings for 2012 showed the group stopped funding all but one organization which had been previously criticized."* (Wikipedia n.d.)

How do we respond? We have a right to be angry about the actions of those who ignore the Law of the LORD, especially those who say they are followers of Christ. Yet, even in our anger we are obligated to bear the image and likeness of our Creator in our response to that anger. What is the proper response? We can take our cue from the psalmist and remember that our pilgrimage here on Earth is temporary, and any time of darkness is also temporary so we are not to be overwhelmed. Yet, we are to set the standard for the culture. We are to live our lives in such a way that the earth begins to resemble the Kingdom of Heaven. Earth will never resemble Heaven until the people of God are unified in bearing the image and likeness of God here on Earth. As the wisdom of proverbs tells us *"When it goes well with the righteous, the city rejoices, and when the wicked perish, there is joyful shouting." "By the blessing of the upright a city is exalted, but by the mouth of the wicked it is torn down." Pro 11:10- 11*

Another key thing to remember is knowing how to praise God in any situation. Our praises are not reserved just for the joyful moments in our lives. Many of the Psalms voice the praises of God in the midst of turmoil. The writers did not let the condition of the culture effect their decision to remain true to the word of God. The writer of Psalm 119 made it a practice to remember, observe, and take delight in God's word.

When we make it a habit to seek God's word for instruction and guidance it's easy to follow His precepts. I leave you with this word of exhortation...

"10 Finally, be strong in the Lord and in the strength of His might. 11 Put on the full armor of God, so that you will be able to stand firm against the schemes of the devil. 12 For our struggle is not against flesh and blood, but against the rulers, against the powers, against the world forces of this darkness, against the spiritual forces of wickedness in the heavenly places. 13 Therefore, take up the full armor of God, so that you will be able to resist in the evil day, and having done everything, to stand firm. 14 Stand firm therefore, HAVING GIRDED YOUR LOINS WITH TRUTH, and HAVING PUT ON THE BREASTPLATE OF RIGHTEOUSNESS, 15 and having shod YOUR FEET WITH THE PREPARATION OF THE GOSPEL OF PEACE; 16 in addition to all, taking up the shield of faith with which you will be able to extinguish all the flaming arrows of the evil one. 17 And take THE HELMET OF SALVATION, and the sword of the Spirit, which is the word of God. 18 With all prayer and petition pray at all times in the Spirit, and with this in view, be on the alert with all perseverance and petition for all the saints," Ephesians 6:10-18 NASB

Praying Psalm 119:49-56

Zayin ז

Prayer Focus

Hope and comfort in God's word

⁴⁹ Remember the word to Your servant, In which You have made me hope.
⁵⁰ This is my comfort in my affliction, That Your word has revived me.

Prayer Focus

Unwavering zeal for the Law of the Lord

⁵¹ The arrogant utterly deride me, Yet I do not turn aside from Your law.
⁵² I have remembered Your ordinances from of old, O LORD, And comfort myself.
⁵³ Burning indignation has seized me because of the wicked, who forsake Your law.

Prayer Focus

Spiritual consistency

⁵⁴ Your statutes are my songs In the house of my pilgrimage.
⁵⁵ O LORD, I remember Your name in the night, And keep Your law.
⁵⁶ This has become mine, That I observe Your precepts.

Creative Challenge *(optional)*

The arrogant utterly deride me, yet I do not turn aside from Your law
Psalm 119:51

Write a story or dialogue about this image. Consider the following questions: How do you think the girl on the right feels? How do the other two girls feel...about the girl or about themselves? Can you identify with any of them? How would you counsel each girl? There is no wrong way to approach this challenge. Think about all you have learned and discussed thus far.

SESSION TEN

HETH

ח

Creativity Page

Welcome back! We are drawing near to the end of our first 12 weeks. I pray this journey has been satisfying, challenging, and informative. Once again, grab your pens, pencils, and a cup of your favorite beverage and join me as we continue our journey through Psalm 119.

Review

☐ What did you learn about anger and righteous indignation? Is there a difference?

Getting Started

☐ What is the difference between being dissatisfied and being unsatisfied? Give some examples.

☐ What are some qualities you look for in establishing personal or business relationships with people or groups?

Read Psalm 119:57-64

57 The LORD is my portion; I have promised to keep Your words.

58 I sought Your favor with all *my* heart; be gracious to me according to Your word.

59 I considered my ways and turned my feet to Your testimonies.

60 I hastened and did not delay to keep Your commandments.

61 The cords of the wicked have encircled me, *but* I have not forgotten Your law.

62 At midnight I shall rise to give thanks to You Because Of Your righteous ordinances.

63 I am a companion of all those who fear You, and of those who keep Your precepts.

64 The earth is full of Your loving kindness, O LORD; teach me Your statutes.

In Psalm 119:57, the psalmist declares the LORD is his portion. The word "portion" can refer to one's share or inheritance they are to receive. The psalmist seems to declare his satisfaction with the LORD being his portion. Let's discuss the idea of being satisfied.

1. What are some things that can cause you to be dissatisfied in life?

2. How does comparing yourself to others affect your satisfaction level?

Word and Word

In Psalm 119: 57, 58 the psalmist promises to keep God's words and then he asks God to be gracious according His word.

Using a concordance or internet word study tool such as **www.blueletterbible.org** to look up the Hebrew rendering of these two variation of the word "word". What do you learn?

Read: Numbers 18:20-24; Deuteronomy 18:1

3. What do you learn about the Levite's portion or inheritance?

Read: Psalm 61:4-5; I Peter 1:3-4

4. What do you learn about your inheritance?

5. How does that affect your ability to be content?

Read: Psalm 119:57-58; Philippians 4:11-13; Proverbs 15:16; 16:8

6. According to the above verses, what are some principles to being content?

7. Take a moment to create bar chart rating your level of contentment in the areas listed. How do feel about what you see?

bar chart example

Life Contentment At-a-Glance

10	
9	
8	
7	
6	
5	
4	
3	
2	
1	

Health   Finances   Career/Education   Relationship   Family   Spiritual Life   Social Life   Self-Image   Purpose

8. There is a practical law of action that says when you encounter a problem, you can either complain or create a solution. If you see your contentment is low in a certain area, what changes do you need to make in that area? What solutions can you create to achieve greater contentment?

9. Looking at the context of psalm 119: 59- 60, what does the psalmist mean by saying he considered his ways?

10. What was his next call to action?

Self-Examination

11. *II Corinthians 13:5* exhorts us to "*Test yourselves to see if you are in the faith; examine yourselves! Or do you not recognize this about yourselves, that Jesus Christ is in you – unless indeed you fail the test?*"

What are some areas in our lives that we should examine or consider our ways? Read the following passages and discuss some of these areas. Can you add to the list?

☐ *John 13:34-35; I John 2:7-11*

☐ *Philippians 4:8-9*

☐ *Romans 8:16; I John 2:1-6, 3:4-10, 24*

☐ *John 15:5, 16; Colossians 1:10*

☐ *Other Areas:*

12. How often do you take the time to consider your path? What is your process for this?

Read: *Psalm 119: 59-60; Lamentations 3:40, II Chronicles 7:14; I John 1:9*
  13. What is the prescription when we find errors in our ways?

14. We know the importance of early detection and urgent treatment of illnesses when it comes to our physical health. How necessary is urgency when applying the remedy for sin? Why?

We know we are all prone to err in our walk with the Word. Let's take a look at how our relationship choices can affect our walk.

Read: *Psalm 1:1; I Corinthians 5:9-13; II Corinthians 6:14; Proverb 2:20; 13:20*

14. In psalm 119:63, the psalmist talks about choosing his companions. Why is it important to choose our relationships wisely?

15. What are some dangers to unwise personal and business relationship choices? Can you share a personal testimony of a time when your choices had a positive or negative impact?

16. List some positive and negative qualities we should consider when building personal and business relationships. How can these qualities affect us and our relationship with God?

Desirable Qualities	Effect	Undesirable Qualities	Effect
Ex: honesty	Mutual trust	Dishonesty	Suspicions

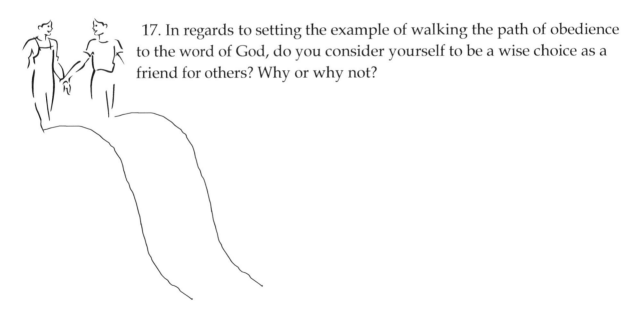

17. In regards to setting the example of walking the path of obedience to the word of God, do you consider yourself to be a wise choice as a friend for others? Why or why not?

Psalm 119:59-60
I considered my ways and turned my feet to Your testimonies.
I hastened and did not delay to keep Your commandments

Time Delay

What are some dangers in delaying obedience? Think about what happened to the Children of Israel during their journey to Canaan. You can read this account in *Numbers 13 and 14*

What happens when you partially obey? Read about what happened to Saul in *I Samuel 15.*

In the blank space draw a clock (you can just draw a plain circle if you wish). List what you have learned from the Children of Israel and Saul in or around the clock.

Remember, this is your time for creative expression. There is no right or wrong way to do these creative applications. Go to the DevArtJournal Community to see and share creative exercises.
www.coachlaurabrown.com

Turning Your Feet

Are there any areas in your life where you are guilty of delaying obedience or being partially obedient to the commandments or words of the LORD? Take this time to pray and consider your ways. Ask God to show you areas where you have strayed due to delayed or partial obedience.

You can use the journal space on this page and/or the space on the next page to record your response

DevArtJournal

Psalm 119:59-60
I considered my ways and turned my feet to Your testimonies.
I hastened and did not delay to keep Your commandments.

Turning Your Feet

Are there any areas in your life where you are guilty of delaying obedience or being partially obedient to the commandments or words of the LORD?

Take this time to pray and consider your ways. Ask God to show you areas where you have strayed due to delayed or partial obedience.

Praying Psalm 119:57-64

Heth ח

Prayer Focus
Satisfaction found in God's word

57 The LORD is my portion; I have promised to keep Your words.
58 I sought Your favor with all *my* heart; Be gracious to me according to Your word.

Prayer Focus
Wisdom of self-examination and repentance

59 I considered my ways And turned my feet to Your testimonies.
60 I hastened and did not delay To keep Your commandments.
61 The cords of the wicked have encircled me, *But* I have not forgotten Your law.

Prayer Focus
Praising God for the wisdom of His word

62 At midnight I shall rise to give thanks to You Because of Your righteous ordinances.

Prayer Focus
Wisdom in building godly relationships

63 I am a companion of all those who fear You, And of those who keep Your precepts.
64 The earth is full of Your loving kindness, O LORD; Teach me Your statutes.

SESSION ELEVEN

TETH

ט

Creativity Page

W elcome back! As we round out our study of Psalm 119, we will be discussing some least
desirable aspects of delighting in the law of the LORD. I want you to keep in mind what
we have learned about the purpose of God's laws at the onset of this study. Remember,
every command, statute, and law flows from the heart of God and represents His character,
His love for His creation and His desire for us to walk in His likeness and image.

Review

☐ What is one principle to being content?

Getting Started

☐ As a child what were the consequences of being disobedient to your
parents/guardians?

☐ How did you feel about those consequences?

☐ Why do you have rules in your household?

☐ If you are a parent, how do you handle disobedience with your children? If you are not
a parent yet, how do you think parents should handle disobedience with their children?

Read Psalm 119:65-72

65 You have dealt well with Your servant, O LORD, according to Your word.

66 Teach me good discernment and knowledge, for I believe in Your commandments.

67 Before I was afflicted I went astray, but now I keep Your word.

68 You are good and do well; teach me Your statutes.

69 The arrogant have forged a lie against me; with all my heart I will observe Your precepts.

70 Their heart is covered with fat, but I delight in Your law.

71 It is good for me that I was afflicted, that I may learn Your statutes.

72 The law of Your mouth is better to me than thousands of gold and silver pieces

1. What does the psalmist acknowledge in Psalm 119: 65, 68, and 72?

Ways

Strong's H1870 - *derek*

1. **manner, habit, way**
2. **direction**
3. **of moral character (fig.)**

2. What does he ask for in Psalm 119:66?

Read: Genesis 1:26; I Kings 3:9; Isaiah 11:2-4; Philippians 1:9; James 3:13-18

3. As a leader (we are all leaders in some aspect), why are discernment and knowledge important?

4. In Psalm 119:67, 71, to what does the writer attribute his willingness to submit to God's word?

Read: Job 5:18; Isaiah 30:26; Hosea 6:1; Deuteronomy 32:39

5. What is one source of our affliction?

6. Read Psalm 119: 67, 71 and discuss the psalmist's response to the result of the affliction that comes from the LORD?

> *Remember the meaning of the word "statutes"? It simply means prescribed boundaries or limitations. The word of God teaches us His boundaries for His children.*

Read: Job 5:17-18; Proverbs 3:11-12; Hebrews 12:5-11
7. What should our response be to chastisement from the LORD? Why?

8. What has been your response when you have experienced correction that you felt was from the LORD and caused by your straying from His prescribed boundaries. Were you joyful, angry, fearful, humbled, etc...? Why?

9. What kind of people does the psalmist talk about in Psalm 119:69-70?

10. What is his response to them?

Read: *Deuteronomy 8:11-18; Isaiah 6:10; Psalm 17:10; Acts 28:27; Revelation 3:17*

11. What are the symptoms and prognosis (probable outcome) of having a "fat" heart left untreated? Use the heart shapes to record your answers.

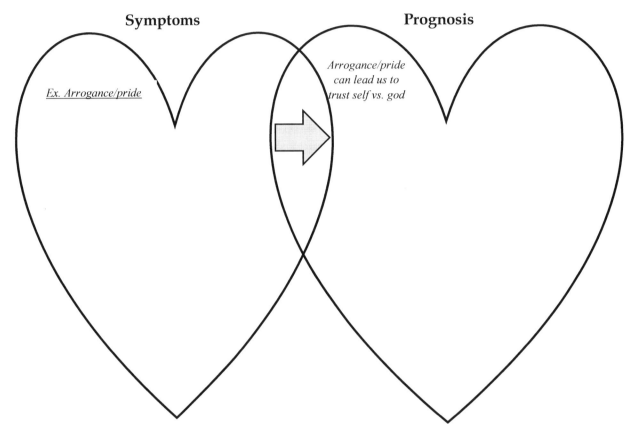

Symptoms

Ex. Arrogance/pride

Prognosis

Arrogance/pride can lead us to trust self vs. god

12. Summarize the meaning of a heart that is covered with fat. Give some modern-day examples.

13. Reread Psalm 119: 65-72. Take note of what the psalmist says is well, good or better. How is the word of God related to these ideas?

DevArtJournal

The arrogant have forged a lie against me; with all my heart I will observe Your precepts.
Their heart is covered with fat, but I delight in Your law.

Heart Condition

Earlier we discussed the signs and dangers of a heart covered with fat. The psalmist also talks about the conditions of his own heart in the midst of persecution, trial, and affliction. Think about the differences of those two heart conditions.
Use this space to compare and contrast the differences of the heart conditions.
You are not limited to using shapes. Dig deep into the creative recesses of your heart and mind to create a picture that speaks volumes about the two heart conditions.

This would be a great one to share with the DevArtJounal Community!
www.coachlaurabrown.com

Change My Heart

As you think about the heart conditions discussed can you relate to one or both of them?

How can delighting in the law of Lord prevent a fattened heart?

What are your strengths and challenges in submitting your heart to the law of the Lord during trial, affliction, or persecution?

Name at least one change you need to make in regards to how you respond to affliction, persecution, or trials.

Change my heart oh God,

Make it ever true.

Change my heart oh God,

May I be like You.

You are the potter,

I am the clay,

Mold me and make me,

This is what I pray.

Author: Eddie Espinosa

The Good Shepherd

Psalm 119:67
Before I was afflicted I went astray, but now I keep Your word.

You may have heard the story of the good shepherd who will break a wayward sheep's leg to keep it from wandering off, and then carry that sheep to teach it the love and care and of a good shepherd. While that story paints a memorable picture of a loving shepherd-God who desires to keep His flock safe, it is not based on verifiable biblical or practical proof. It is a retelling of story, a fable perhaps, that has been retold numerous times to the point of it being regarded as truth. During my investigation of the source of this story, I came across the following explanation on **www.christianforums.com** from writer, "jeolmstead". This is a response from a present-day sheepherder when asked if a shepherd would break a wayward sheep's leg:

> *"It is not true that any shepherds break a lamb's leg on purpose.*
>
> *What they sometimes do in certain sheep-raising nations is to "brake" a leg. This means they attach a clog or weight to the animal's leg, which keeps certain "rogue" sheep from getting too far from the shepherd until they learn their names, and not to be afraid of the shepherd.*
>
> *Rogue sheep are those that won't stay with the flock--important to their safety. A single sheep that constantly moves out and away from the others is the certain target of predators, and often is at risk of wandering out of sight (over a hill, into the brush, etc.) in terrain where the shepherd is unable to count the sheep properly. Then the sheep would be surely lost.*
>
> *Each shepherd looks after from about 1200 to 3000 sheep. When they're constantly moving, such large numbers are impossible to count with precision.*
>
> *To keep track of such large numbers of sheep, they must be corralled, and then " passed under the rod," which means the shepherd has them in a narrow chute that enables each sheep to be counted one by one, and even marked with paint, charcoal, etc., for further work if necessary.*
>
> *The leg brake is a temporary measure; a lamb with a braked leg (it's not a "broken" leg!) is still easy pickings for predators at night, because it can't run as fast as the flock when under attack, and shepherd usually can't see predators in the dark.*
>
> *Yours,*
>
> *Nathan Griffith, editor*
>
> *Sheep! Magazine"*

What does this teach us? One thing it teaches us is to remember that when we, as wayward sheep, go astray, it invites difficulty and hardships to come into our lives. The danger we put ourselves in when we decide to leave the safety and boundaries of the great

Shepherd's presence grieves Him. Because He loves and cares for His sheep, He will use temporary measures to get our attention and oft times those are not pleasant experiences. We can and should use those moments to teach us not to stray from the paths of God's word. He has given us boundaries in His word for our safety. Even though He will not "break" our legs, He may "brake" us with affliction to hinder our wandering into paths of destruction and turn us back onto the path of life. Remember, His boundaries and His reproof flow from the love He has for His children "For whom the LORD loves He reproves, Even as a father corrects the son in whom he delights." *(Proverbs 3:12)* Our response should be as the psalmist who recognizes the benefits of God's loving correction. Paul states in *Hebrews 12:11*, "All discipline for the moment seems not to be joyful, but sorrowful; yet to those who have been trained by it, afterwards it yields the peaceful fruit of righteousness." Delighting in the law of the LORD will take learning to delight in His correction also.

Praying Psalm 119:65-72

Teth ט

Prayer Focus
Desire to be taught the LORD

65 You have dealt well with Your servant, O LORD, according to Your word.
66 Teach me good discernment and knowledge, For I believe in Your commandments.

Prayer Focus
Learning the proper response to Godly correction

67 Before I was afflicted I went astray, But now I keep Your word.
68 You are good and do good; Teach me Your statutes.

Prayer Focus
Delighting in the word in the during trials

69 The arrogant have forged a lie against me; With all my heart I will observe Your precepts.
70 Their heart is covered with fat, But I delight in Your law.

Prayer Focus
Valuing the law of the LORD

71 It is good for me that I was afflicted, That I may learn Your statutes.
72 The law of Your mouth is better to me Than thousands of gold and silver pieces.

Creativity Page

SESSION TWELVE

YOD

‘

Creativity Page

We have arrived at the end of our first 12-week journey in Delighting in the Law of the LORD. I pray that you have been blessed, informed, and challenged. Plan on spending some extra time working on this session's discussion questions. Pray for wisdom and the ability to hear the Father's loving voice, and feel His presence as you work through the lesson. Grab your colored pencils, that cup of coffee or tea, and take a deep breath and dive into the delight of the Law of the LORD.

Review

☐ What is the meaning of the word ways?

Getting Started

☐ When purchasing a new product, how important is it to read the manufacturer's warranty?

☐ What are some stipulations commonly contained in a warranty (ex. technology, appliances, vehicles, etc.)

☐ What happens if the terms of the warranty are violated?

Read Psalm 119:73-80 – *Remember to record your notes about the different words referring to the law in the table in the appendix. If you have been color coding throughout the study it will be easy to go back and record the ones you may have forgotten to annotate.*

73 Your hands made me and fashioned me; Give me understanding, that I may learn Your commandments.

74 May those who fear You see me and be glad, because I wait for Your word.

75 I know, O LORD, that Your judgments are righteous, and that in faithfulness You have afflicted me.

76 O may your loving kindness comfort me, According to Your word to Your servant.

77 May Your compassion come to me that I may live, For Your law is my delight.

78 May the arrogant be ashamed, for they subvert me with a lie; but I shall meditate on Your precepts.

79 May those who fear You turn to me, even those who know Your testimonies.

80 May my heart be blameless in Your statutes, So that I will not be ashamed.

1. What does the psalmist acknowledge in verse 73?

2. What does he ask for in light of that acknowledgement?

3. Why did he ask for it?

Read: *Genesis 1:26-28; Psalm 115:15-16*

4. Since we are created by God, why is it important that we know His commandments?

5. How can we obtain this understanding?

6. Psalm 119: 74, 78, and 79 talks about two types of people. Who are they?

7. What is the difference between them?

8. Why would your trust and obedience in God's word make others either joyful or wrathful?

Read: I Corinthians 11:1, 4:6; Philippians 3:17; Hebrews 13:7; II Timothy 1:13, 2:1-2

9. How much importance should you place on how others view your relationship with God and His word? Why?

Read: Proverbs 11:10-11; 28:12; 29:2

10. What impact can your actions have on others in: your family, your neighborhood, your job, your city, your church? You can choose to use the space below to create an image which portrays the impact of the righteous and of the wicked.

During our last session we discussed the necessity and benefit of correction by a loving God. We will revisit that discussion in the next three verses. Our focus will not be on the reality of the correction but the reason God cannot allow us to continue down a path of destruction.

11. In Psalm 119:75, what does the psalmist recognize?

12. **Word study review:** What does the word judgment represent? (Think about a court room)

13. Do you recall what you learned regarding the purpose of God's laws? If not, take a moment to review the information from our first session. How does God's faithfulness relate to the reason He corrects us?

Read: *Deuteronomy 28:1-15; Exodus 19:5-6; Isaiah 6:3*

14. To what is God obligated to be faithful?

Read: Leviticus 11:45; I Peter 1:14-15; I Thessalonians 4:1-8; Hebrew 13:7-8; Revelations 4:8

15. How has God's character changed over time?

16. What insight do you get about what is expected in regards to your character?

Read: *Exodus 19:5-6; I Peter 2:9; Revelations 1:4-6; 5:7-10*

17. Why is it important that we remain teachable and open to correction?

18. Is there a difference between punishment and correction in regards to purpose, methods and outcomes of each? Hebrews 12 is a good place to start. Use a Venn Diagram to compare and contrast them. Use a blank sheet of paper if you need more space. See example on page 167 in the appendix.

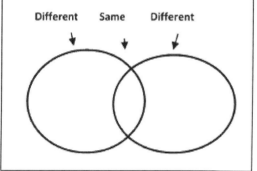

Venn Diagrams

Venn Diagrams are visual representations that show the similarities and differences between concepts. They can be created by overlapping two (or more) shapes. You then list the characteristics or attributes of the concepts, ideas, or topics in the corresponding shapes. Those characteristics which are shared are listed in the overlapping portion of the shape.

19. Summarize your answer to question number 18.

20. What can we hope for from God in the aftermath of His correction? Provide supporting scripture.

21. How does that help you to receive correction?

22. How can you use this information to guide you when you must give correction to others?

Take a moment to pray and thank God for loving you enough to correct you and for the wisdom and ability to respond to His correction with joy and hope for restoration.

23. What is the psalmist's desire for the arrogant in Psalm 119:78? Why?

24. What is his response?

25. What are precepts?

Delightful Wisdom

When a man's ways are pleasing to the LORD, He makes even his enemies to be at peace with him. *with him.*

Proverbs 16:7

Read the story of King David and his experience with someone who was arrogant. This man was Shimei who met David along the road as he was in the process of losing his throne to his own son. Take special note on David's response. You can find this account in *II Samuel 16:1-13 and 19:16-23.*

How does this story relate to *Psalm 119:78?*

26. How can knowing godly precepts help you to handle difficult situations or people?

27. What is his final request in Psalm 119:80? Why?

28. Before whom doesn't the psalmist want to be ashamed?

Read: II Timothy 2:15; I John 2:27-29; 4:13-18; Psalm 119:1

29. What is our responsibility to ensure our hearts are blameless before God and man?

Read: Matthew 22:35-40

30. What solution does Jesus give for remaining blameless before God and man?

31. What is the central principle to Jesus' solution?

Exodus 20:3-17

It has been said that if you cannot explain something to a six year old then you don't understand it well enough yourself. As we have discussed the law of the LORD in regards to its meaning, origin, purpose, and our relationship with it do you think you understand enough to explain to a child?

Your assignment this week is to rewrite the Ten Commandments using language a child would understand.

If you are daring to be creative draw visual representations of each commandment

All Scripture is inspired by God and profitable for teaching, for reproof, for correction, for training in righteousness;
so that the man of God may be adequate, equipped for every good work.
II Timothy 3:16-17

As we end the first twelve weeks of studying Psalm 119 take a moment to think about what has been your greatest reward from your time with this Psalm. What has encouraged you, challenged you, comforted you, or motivated you the most?

Praying Psalm 119:73-80

Yod ׳

Prayer Focus
*Beauty of those who follow and wait
On the LORD*

73 Your hands made me and fashioned me; Give me understanding, that I may learn Your commandments.

74 May those who fear You see me and be glad, Because I wait for Your word.

Prayer Focus
Comfort in the word of God

75 I know, O LORD, that Your judgments are righteous, And that in faithfulness You have afflicted me.

76 O may Your loving kindness comfort me, According to Your word to Your servant.

77 May Your compassion come to me that I may live, For Your law is my delight.

Prayer Focus
The vindicating Word of God

78 May the arrogant be ashamed, for they subvert me with a lie; But I shall meditate on Your precepts.

79 May those who fear You turn to me, Even those who know Your testimonies.

Prayer Focus
*Living without shame before man
And God*

80 May my heart be blameless in Your statutes, So that I will not be ashamed.

Reading the Fine Print

When a manufacturer creates a product they expect it to function as designed. There are "laws" built into it to assure its proper function. When the product malfunctions it is a sign that a "law" of operation has been violated. When you purchase a product, it is important to know and heed those "laws" in order to ensure the item functions at its optimum best.

Most warranties will stipulate that the manufacturer shall not be held responsible for malfunctions due to violation of the laws of operation. This means that the warranty, and any right to return the item, is made void. Our Creator God, on the other hand, takes responsibility and care of His creation, even when we violate the law, as long as we return to our original design of His likeness and image. He reminds us to "be holy as He is holy", we are "kings and priest", we are "a holy nation" We are reminded in *Ephesians 2:10* that, "we are His workmanship, created in Christ Jesus for good works, which God prepared beforehand so that we would walk in them". Genesis through Revelation is replete with exhortation to live in holiness and righteousness as we were originally created.

Not only does God desire us to live as He originally designed, He gave us clear instructions on how to do it. He provided us ways to be restored when we fail. In the Old Testament those methods of restoration were through continual blood sacrifices of animals.

On the other hand, those who have chosen to accept Jesus, the ultimate blood sacrifice, as savior and Lord, have been given the Holy Spirit to lead and guide us according to the spirit of God's laws. Even when we violate the law, we have the ability and access to receive restoration through acknowledging our sins and repenting (which means to stop and turn around, go back to our original design!).

Read the fine print in *I John 1:9*

"If we confess our sins, He is faithful and righteous to forgive us our sins and to cleanse us from all unrighteousness."

Read the fine print. There is a repentance that leads to salvation

"Therefore repent and return, so that your sins may be wiped away, in order that times of refreshing may come from the presence of the Lord; and that He may send Jesus, the Christ appointed for you" (Acts 3:19-20)

Read the fine print. There is a repentance that leads to restoration

"Those whom I love, I reprove and discipline; therefore be zealous and repent. Behold, I stand at the door and knock; if anyone hears My voice and opens the door, I will come in to him and will dine with him, and he with Me." (Revelation 3:19-20)

It should be our desire, as people who are made in the image and likeness of God, to remain in a state of restoration. We do that by following godly laws and precepts, which Jesus summed by saying *"you shall love the Lord your God with all your heart, and with all your soul, and with all your mind.' 38 "this is the great and foremost commandment. 39 "the second is like it, 'you shall love your neighbor as yourself.' 40 "on these two commandments depend the whole law and the prophets." (Mat 22:37-40).*

Abiding by God's laws should be enjoyable because of the results. The results are peace and order in our lives. The results are living our lives without shame before man, and knowing that when we stand before God we have no fear of being ashamed before Him. We will stand as mighty conquerors and receive the fruit of obedience

"He who overcomes will thus be clothed in white garments; and I will not erase his name from the book of life, and I will confess his name before My Father and before His angels. He who has an ear, let him hear what the Spirit says to the churches." Revelation 3:5-6

I stand in whole-hearted agreement that you are an overcomer because you have chosen to delight in the law of the Lord!

The Conclusion of the Matter

Wisdom is the principal thing; therefore get wisdom: and with all thy getting get understanding.
Proverbs 4:7 (KJV)

In the space below, summarize how this study has impacted your understanding and acquisition of the wisdom in delighting in the law of the LORD. You can write or draw your response.

Creativity Page

Appendix

If I remember correctly, the ladies of the Pregnancy Care Center (PCC) were praying for each other during our group prayer time, and we spoke these words verbally over each other after our personal DevArtio time was over.

Law Table

Use this chart to keep track of what you learn about the different words, which refer to various aspects of the Law. Write a short working definition under the word and short statement about what Psalm 119 says about them in the right column. See the examples below. (Sometimes you may encounter a word with no information to add about it). Feel free to tear these pages out, along with the theme chart on page 166 to make it easier to keep track of the information.

Law	*Ex. blesses those who walk in it (1)*
Testimonies	*Ex. blessed are those who keep it (2)*
Ways	*Ex. walk in it to avoid sin (3)*

Precepts	Ex. keep them diligently (4)
Statutes	Ex. direct our ways to keep them to prevent shame (5)
Commandments	Ex. don't wander from them (10)

Judgments	*Ex. we should long for them (20)*
Word	*Ex. keeps our way clean (9)*

Psalm 119 Theme Chart

Verses	Themes	Notes
Aleph **1-8**		
Beth **9-16**		
Gimel **17-24**		
Daleth **25-32**		
He **33-40**		
Vav **41-48**		
Zayin **49-56**		
Heth **57-64**		
Teth **65-72**		
Yod **72-80**		

Venn Diagram

Venn Diagrams are visual representations that show relationship and the similarities and differences between two or more concepts. They are created by overlapping two or more shapes. You then list the characteristics or attributes of the concepts, ideas, or topics in the corresponding shapes. The characteristics which are shared are listed in the overlapping portion of the shape. Each section can be shaded a different color.

Example: Show the relationship between mammals and fish.

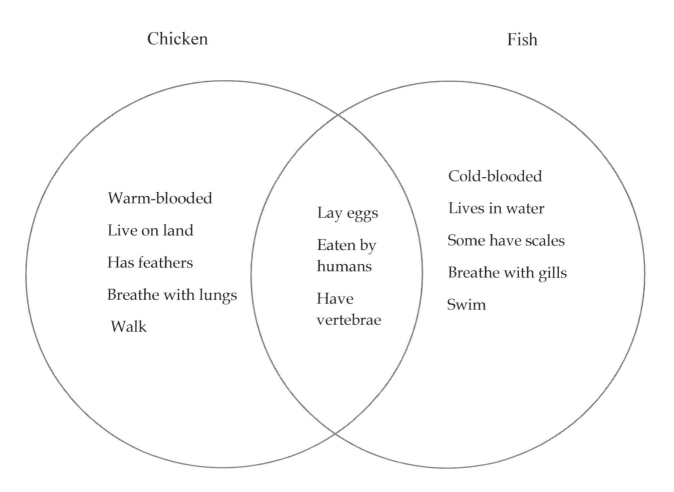

Chicken

Fish

Warm-blooded

Live on land

Has feathers

Breathe with lungs

Walk

Lay eggs

Eaten by humans

Have vertebrae

Cold-blooded

Lives in water

Some have scales

Breathe with gills

Swim

WORD STUDY INSTRUCTIONS

*Tools Needed: Study Bible, several recent translations (not paraphrased), exhaustive concordance, bible dictionary/encyclopedia, a set of word studies, English dictionary. **On-line resources for above:***

www.studylight.org; www.blueletterbible.org; www.biblos.com; www.biblegateway.com

1. VERSE (circle or highlight word you want to study)	

2. ENGLISH DEFINITIOIN:	3. COMPARE TRANSLATIONS:

4. SHORT HEBREW/GREEK DEFINITON (include Strong's number):

5. OCCURANCES IN THE BIBLE:
  - TIMES USED:
  - BOOKS THAT USE IT
  - MOST OCCURANCES
  - FIRST OCCURANCE IN THE BIBLE:
  - FIRST OCCURANCE IN THE BOOK I'M STUDYING:

6. LONGER STRONG'S DEFINITION *(if available):*

7. WORD USAGE IN THE BIBLE…how the word was used is most important factor to determine true meaning

  1. How is the word translated into English every time it appears? (*Use exhaustive concordance or on-line tools)*

  2. How does the writer use it in other parts of this book?

  3. How does the writer use it in other books he has written?

  4. How is used throughout the whole Testament?

  5. How is it used the <u>first</u> time in the scripture?

  6. What is the <u>most frequent</u> use of the word?

  7. What would we know about this topic if this verse was the only mention of it?

  8. What is the correlating Greek word?

  9. *How is the word used in the context of this passage? (Does the context give any clues? Is it compared or contrasted with another word? Any illustrations to clarify it?)*

8. BACK TO THE VERSE; Reread the verse using the expanded definition. Does it add light to the verse? How?

9. APPLICATION/IN YOUR OWN WORDS: Remember, the goal of ANY study is personal application. Ask yourself "How can understanding this word strengthen my life?"

10. NOTES FOR FURTHER STUDY:

11. RESOURCE(S)

WORD STUDY WORKSHEET EXAMPLE

<table>
<tr>
<td colspan="3">

1. VERSE (circle or highlight word you want to study)

Then God said, "Let Us make man in Our image, H6754 according to Our likeness; H1823 and let them rule over the fish of the sea and over the birds of the sky and over the cattle and over all the earth, and over every creeping thing that creeps on the earth."

</td>
</tr>
<tr>
<td>

2. ENGLISH DEFINITIOIN: IMAGE

- Actual or mental picture
- Likeness seen or produced

- Somebody closely resembling somebody else

</td>
<td>

ENGLISH DEFINITIOIN: LIKENESS

- Representation of somebody or something often considered in terms of accurately it represents the person or thing.

- Similarity of appearance

</td>
<td>

3. COMPARE TRANSLATIONS: No significant difference

</td>
</tr>
<tr>
<td>

4. SHORT HEBREW/GREEK DEFINITON (include Strong's number): H6754 - *tselem - masculine noun*

1. image
    1. images (of tumors, mice, heathen gods)
    2. image, likeness (of resemblance)
    3. mere, empty, image, semblance (fig.)

</td>
<td colspan="2">

SHORT HEBREW/GREEK DEFINITON H1823 – dĕmuwth (dem·üth) adverb, feminine noun

n f

   likeness, similitude

adv.

   in the likeness of, like as

</td>
</tr>
<tr>
<td>

5. OCCURANCES IN THE BIBLE:
- image (16x)
- vain shew (1x)
- used first in Gen. 1:26
- Genesis, I Samuel, 2 Kings, 2 Chron., Psalms (vain shew) & Ezekiel

</td>
<td colspan="2">

5.   OCCURANCES IN THE BIBLE:
- Likeness (19x)
- Similitude (2x)
- Like (2x)
- Manner (1x)
- Fashion (1x)

</td>
</tr>
<tr>
<td colspan="3">

6. LONGER STRONG'S DEFINITION *(if available):*

</td>
</tr>
<tr>
<td>

7. WORD USAGE IN THE BIBLE...how the word was used is most important factor to determine true meaning

  a. When God created man He used the word image to mean like Him (Gen. 1:26-27, 9:6)

  b. Adam fathered Seth according his image (Gen. 5:3)

</td>
<td colspan="2">

7.   **WORD USAGE IN THE BIBLE...**

  a. According to His likeness
  b. Pattern/fashion(2 Kings 16:10)
  c. Figures like oxen (2 Chr. 4:3
  d. Resembling (Eze. 10:1)

</td>
</tr>
</table>

c. Heathens made images of tumors and mice (I Sa 6:5) d. Images referring to false gods (2 Kings 3:17, Eze. 7:20, 16:17, 23:14, Amos 5:26) e. Used as word phantom (vain shew) to mean emptiness (Ps. 39:6)	

8. BACK TO THE VERSE; Reread the verse using the expanded definition. Does it add light to the verse? How?

Then God said, "Let Us make man in Our image, to function and act as we are we functioning and according to Our likeness, with our character and qualities, and let them rule over the fish of the sea and over the birds of the sky and over the cattle and over all the earth, and over every creeping thing that creeps on the earth."

9. APPLICATION/IN YOUR OWN WORDS: Remember, the goal of ANY study is personal application. Ask

- Since God did not possess a body He could not have been referring to our physical image. God is spirit, so He when He said let Us make man in our image He must have been referring to our spirit.

- God wanted to make mankind to resemble what He (They) look like. God is spirit, not flesh, so His idea of creating man focused on our spirits. Flesh was needed to house His creation.

- Likeness seems to be referring to attributes…

- Image and likeness = function and qualities? (Be holy for I am Holy….)

10. NOTES FOR FURTHER STUDY:

In Indo-European languages, *masculine nouns are descended from agent nouns - things that do things. Feminine nouns are descended from adjectival nouns - things that are something.* However, the meanings of words have changed so much in the past five thousand years that the distinction has become obscure. The words for female and male humans take after the nouns, not the other way round, so it's basically because women tended to be thought of in terms of their attributes and men in terms of what they did.

Sometimes, it does make a difference. For instance, in Danish the word "ore" (with a crossed-out O that I don't know how to type) means a kind of coin in one gender but an ear in another. Similarly, in French "un calculateur" is someone who calculates but "une calculatrice" is a pocket calculator.

In other languages, for example Arabic and Hebrew, the gender has other characteristics. **In Hebrew, objects that naturally come in pairs such as eyes and shoes are feminine**. This is similar to the tendency in English to describe single objects which are in some way doubled as if they were plural, such as trousers, scissors and glasses.

askyahoo.com

11. RESOURCE(S)

Blueletterbible.com
Encarta Dictionary

WORD STUDY WORKSHEET

*Tools Needed: study Bible, several recent translations (not paraphrased), exhaustive concordance, bible dictionary/encyclopedia, a set of word studies, English dictionary. **On-line resources for above:***

www.studylight.org; www.blueletterbible.org; www.biblos.com; www.biblegateway.com

1. **VERSE (circle or highlight word you want to study)**	
2. **ENGLISH DEFINITIOIN:**	3. **COMPARE TRANSLATIONS:**
4. **SHORT HEBREW/GREEK DEFINITON (include Strong's number):**	
5. **OCCURANCES IN THE BIBLE:**	
6. **LONGER STRONG'S DEFINITION** *(if available):*	
7. **WORD USAGE IN THE BIBLE…how the word was used is most important factor to determine true meaning**	

8. **BACK TO THE VERSE; Reread the verse using the expanded definition. Does it add light to the verse? How?**

9. **APPLICATION/IN YOUR OWN WORDS: Remember, the goal of ANY study is personal application. Ask**

10. **NOTES FOR FURTHER STUDY:**

11. **RESOURCE(S)**

Heart Monitor

Scripture: _____

1	2	3	4	5	VS	Observation

Prescription (what are you going to do?):

The Commandments and God's Character

We discussed that all of God's commandments flow from His character. Read the commandments below and determine what aspect of God's character it represents.

Commandment	Character
Then God spoke all these words, saying, "I am the LORD your God, who brought you out of the land of Egypt, out of the house of slavery. "You shall have no other gods before Me.	
"You shall not make for yourself an idol, or any likeness of what is in heaven above or on the earth beneath or in the water under the earth. "You shall not worship them or serve them;"	
"You shall not take the name of the LORD your God in vain, for the LORD will not leave him unpunished who takes His name in vain."	
"Remember the Sabbath day, to keep it holy. "Six days you shall labor and do all your work, but the seventh day is a Sabbath of the LORD your God; in it you shall not do any work, you or your son or your daughter, your male or your female servant or your cattle or your sojourner who stays with you."	
"Honor your father and your mother, that your days may be prolonged in the land which the LORD your God gives you."	
"You shall not murder."	
"You shall not commit adultery."	
"You shall not steal."	
"You shall not covet your neighbor's house; you shall not covet your neighbor's wife or his male servant or his female servant or his ox or his donkey or anything that belongs to your neighbor."	

More Scriptures to Use with Creative DevArtio

Bible Gateway Top 100 Scriptures- (Bible Gateway n.d.)

1. John 3:16
2. Jer 29:11
3. Rom 8:28
4. Phil 4:13
5. Gen 1:1
6. Prov 3:5
7. Prov 3:6
8. Rom 12:2
9. Phil 4:6
10. Matt 28:19
11. Eph 2:8
12. Gal 5:22
13. Rom 12:1
14. John 10:10
15. Acts 18:10
16. Acts 18:9
17. Acts 18:11
18. Gal 2:20
19. 1 John 1:9
20. Rom 3:23
21. John 14:6
22. Matt 28:20
23. Rom 5:8
24. Phil 4:8
25. Phil 4:7
26. Josh 1:9
27. Isa 40:31
28. Eph 2:9
29. Rom 6:23
30. Gal 5:23
31. Isa 53:5
32. 1 Pet 3:15
33. 2 Tim 3:16
34. Matt 6:33
35. Heb 12:2
36. 1 Pet 5:7
37. Eph 2:10
38. 1 Cor 10:13
39. Matt 11:28
40. Heb 11:1
41. 2 Cor 5:17
42. Heb 13:5
43. 2 Cor 12:9
44. Rom 10:9
45. Isa 41:10
46. Gen 1:26
47. Matt 11:29
48. John 16:33
49. Acts 1:8
50. 2 Tim 1:7

For more information about Creative Prayer read *Praying in Color* by Sybil MacBeth

Creativity Page

Creativity Page

Creativity Page

DevArtio Examples

Praying the Scriptures

Psalm 119:65

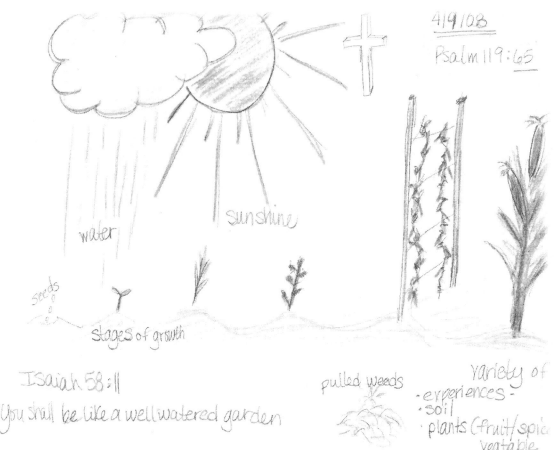

You have dealt well with your servant, O Lord, according to your Word.

Intercessory Prayer Request

These are two examples from different people based on same prayer requests given to our group.

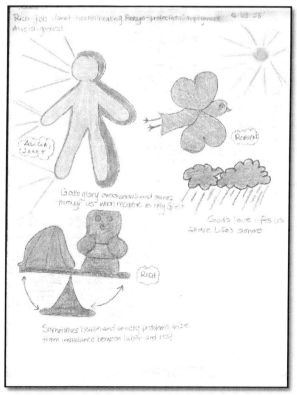

Because of Who You Are

This one is actually an explosion of color as the person was meditating on the awesomeness of Jesus. To see this one and others in full color, go to the DevArtJournal Community at: **www.coachlaurabrown.com.**

Same day of prayer from a different person's perspective!

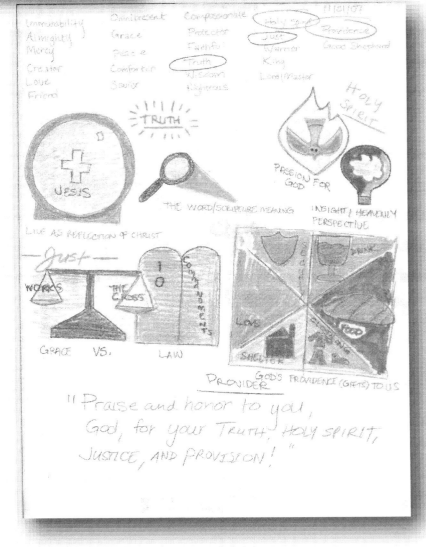

DevArtio with Music

PCC ladies were praying and worshipping with the song "I Cry Holy" by Dennis Jernigan playing softly in the background.

...And I cry, "Holy! Holy! Holy!
Holy is the Lamb who was slain to wash all my guilty stain away!"
And I cry, "Holy! Holy! Holy!
Holy is the Lamb! Holy is the Lamb! Holy is the Lamb!"...

As you can see, there are unlimited ways in which you can creatively express your prayers, love and adoration for the King of kings. There is no one way in which to do this. Go on, grab your rainbow of pens and pencils and enter your quiet time with the Lord with a burst of color!

Creativity Page

Author Recommendations

Reading Resources

Praying in Color- Drawing a New Path to God
Sybil MacBeth

Rick Warren's Bible Study Methods- 12 Ways You Can Unlock God's Word
Rick Warren

Learn to Study the Bible- Forty Different step-by-step methods to help you discover, apply, and enjoy God's Word
Andy Deane

Contemplative Bible Reading- Experiencing God Through Scripture
Richard Peace

Suggested Reference Resources

Concordance- list of every word in the bible with Hebrew and Greek definitions. I recommend the Strong's Concordance

Bible Dictionary

Topical Bible

Bible Handbook

Vine's Expository Dictionary

Bible Maps

Manners and Customs in the Bible

On-Line Study Resources

www.blueletter.org

www.biblegateway.org

www.studylight.org

Smartphone Applications & Computer Software

E-Sword

You Version

Bible Explorer

Lesson Maker 8 Complete

Illumina

Soaking Music

What is soaking music?

Music sung or played characterized by relaxing, peaceful, gentle tones and harmonies.

Prayer Songs Volumes 1-4 – Jeff Nelson

A Prophetic Harp and a Golden Bowl- Michael-David

Prophetic Warrior, Volume I - Instrumental -- by John Belt

You can find other great "soaking" instrumental worship at: **www.elijahlist.com**

There are other resources that are too numerous to mention. These listings are a sampling of my personal favorites.

Works Cited

n.d. *Bible Gateway.* www.biblegateway.org.

n.d. *Bible.org.* www.bible.org.

n.d. *Blue Letter Bible.* www.blueletterbible.org.

Deane, Andy. 2009. *Lean to Study the Bible.* Xulon Press.

J. Hampton Keathley, III. 2004. *How Should New Testament Believers Relate to OT Law.* June 10. Accessed March 2014. www.bible.org.

Keathley, Hampton J. 2004. *The Mosaic Law: Its Function and Purpose in the New Testament.* June 10. Accessed March 2014. www.bible.org.

MacBeth, Sybil. 2007. *Praying in Color.* Brewster: Paraclete Press.

O., John. 2006. *Christian Forums.* August 2006. www.christianforums.com.

Walk with the Word. 1998-2010. *Walk with the Word.* http://www.walkwiththeword.org/Studies/01_OT/19_Psalm/19_Psalm_119.09-16.html.

Warren, Rick. 2006. *Rick Warren's Bible Study Methods.* Grand Rapids: Zondrvan.

Wikipedia. n.d. *Chick-fil-A same-sex marriage controversy.* www. wikepedia.org.

Notes

About the Author

Laura Brown is the founder and coach of "Wells of Truth" Peer-Based Bible Coaching Group, where she teaches students how to study the Bible, by using simple and creative study techniques. She is also a speaker and teacher at The Empowerment Church where she also serves, with her husband Wayne, on the Leadership Team. She has created several home Bible study curriculums that she has used in small-group studies in her home. She is the creator and coach of the Serious Writers' Accountability Training (S.W.A.T.) Camp, which is a writing and publishing camp for aspiring authors. She is the author of "Delighting in the Law of the Lord- Psalm 119 DevArtJournal".

She has a heart to motivate believers, into becoming life-long students of the Bible, by equipping them with tools and techniques, to create a sense of awe and adventure when approaching their devotional and study time in the Word of God.

Laura is a native of Toledo, Ohio and now resides in Chattanooga, TN. She is married to Wayne Brown and they have three children and two grandchildren. Laura enjoys all things creative. Whether designing custom jewelry, coasters, ornaments or meals for family and friends, she relishes in adding her personal touch to her creations. One of her favorite pastimes is dreaming of travel ideas for her husband and her to share with their granddaughters, known as Secret "Pop Pop" and "Nanna" adventures.

If you would like to be on the mailing list, to be notified when Psalm 119 DevArtJounal Part II is available, please email Laura at: **coachlaurabrown@gmail.com.**

To connect with the DevArtJournal community go to: **www.coachlaurabrown.com.**

To learn more about the Serious Writers' Accountability and Training (S.W.A.T.) camp go to: **www.swatbookcamp.com.**

40919645R00117

Made in the USA
Lexington, KY
23 April 2015